EASY
JAPANESE
COOKBOOK

EASY
JAPANESE
COOKBOOK

EMI KAZUKO

THE STEP-BY-STEP GUIDE TO DELICIOUSLY EASY JAPANESE FOOD AT HOME

DUNCAN BAIRD PUBLISHERS

LONDON

Easy Japanese Cookbook
Emi Kazuko

This edition first published in the United Kingdom and Ireland in 2010 by
Duncan Baird Publishers Ltd
Sixth Floor
Castle House
75–76 Wells Street
London W1T 3QH

Conceived, created and designed by Duncan Baird Publishers

Managing Editor: Grace Cheetham
Editors: Nicola Graimes and Alison Bolus
Managing Designer: Suzanne Tuhrim
Designer: Luana Gobbo
Studio Photography: William Lingwood
Stylists: Emi Kazuko (food and props), Atsuko Console
(food stylist assistant) and Helen Trent (props)

British Library Cataloguing-in-Publication Data:
A CIP record for this book is available from the British Library

ISBN: 978-1-84483-933-9

10 9 8 7 6 5 4 3 2 1

Typeset in Spectrum and Univers
Colour reproduction by Scanhouse, Malaysia
Printed in Singapore by Imago

To Dino and Amer, my young Bosnian friends, with love

Author's acknowledgements
I would like to thank all involved with this book at Duncan Baird
Publishers, particularly Grace Cheetham and Suzanne Tuhrim for their
support, Nicola Graimes and Alison Bolus for their painstaking editing,
and Luana Gobbo for designing this beautiful book. My heartfelt thanks
also go to William Lingwood for taking such pretty photographs of my
dishes and to my long-time friend Atsuko Console for assisting me in food
styling for the photography. I am deeply indebted to my food writer
colleague Sallie Morris for recommending me to the publisher, and to my
niece Yuko Kasai for her kind willingness in helping me with my research
in Japan. Above all I owe so much to my late parents, who provided me
with a good foundation in life and food. Thank you.

Publisher's note
While every care has been taken in compiling the recipes for this book,
Duncan Baird Publishers, or any other persons who have been involved in
working on this publication, cannot accept responsibility for any errors or
omissions, inadvertent or not, that may be found in the recipes or text,
nor for any problems that may arise as a result of preparing one of these
recipes. If you are pregnant or breastfeeding or have any special dietary
requirements or medical conditions, it is advisable to consult a medical
professional before following any of the recipes contained in this book. Ill
or elderly people, babies, young children, and women who are pregnant
or breastfeeding should avoid the recipes containing uncooked eggs or
raw meat, fish or seafood.

Notes on the recipes
When preparing any recipe that contains raw fish, always ensure the fish
is very fresh.

Unless otherwise stated:
• Use medium eggs
• Use fresh herbs
• Do not mix metric and imperial measurements
• 1 tsp = 5ml • 1 tbsp = 15ml • 1 cup = 250ml

CONTENTS

INTRODUCTION   6

PART 1   THE BASICS 8

Ingredients   10
Techniques   19
Equipment   23
Basic Recipes   24

PART 2   THE RECIPES 32

Appetizers and Starters   34
Soups   66
Sushi and Sashimi   76
Main Courses   104
Salads and Vegetables   136
Rice and Noodles   154
Desserts   170

PART 3   THE MENUS 186

Simple Lunch   188
Lunch Box   190
Mid-week Lunch with Family   192
Mid-week Lunch with Friends   194
Weekend Lunch with Family   196
Weekend Lunch with Friends   198
Simple Dinner   200
Romantic Dinner   202
Mid-week Dinner with Family   204
Mid-week Dinner with Friends   206
Dinner Party   208
Drinks Party   210

INDEX   212

INTRODUCTION

What distinguishes Japanese cooking from many other cuisines in the world is its sheer simplicity. It is vital in Japan to appreciate and value the natural taste and texture of fresh produce, and the best way to do this is to cook ingredients gently and simply, for the minimum amount of time feasible. Strong herbs and spices are largely unused since they can mask the natural flavour of foods. Furthermore, the meticulous detail the Japanese display in many areas of their lives, from painting to microchip production, is equally evident in their style of cooking, from the preparation of a dish to its exquisite presentation – this is at the heart of the Japanese philosophy of eating.

Japanese cuisine had largely been the hidden treasure of the culinary world until sushi broke the mould and became a phenomenon that swept many parts of the world in the early nineties. Along with Japan's increasing international importance, there has been a steady growth in Japanese restaurants and food stores in many major cities in the West, and the influx of *kaiten-zushi* (sushi served on conveyer belts) made otherwise very expensive Japanese food more accessible to the general public. The last of the world's most mysterious cuisines was thus finally unveiled, and now the West is finding that there is much more to Japanese cooking than sushi and tempura.

Japan is about the size of Britain, with a population of around 125 million. Geographically, it stretches through 16 degrees of latitude: a distance equal to that between northern Scotland and southern France, and the local produce varies accordingly. Moreover, it is a mountainous country, with huge mountain ranges running through the centre from north to south, covering some 75–80 per cent of the landmass. The produce, as a result, varies not only by season and region but also by altitude, ranging from the high mountains to the plains running along the coast. Also, the clash of warm and cold currents makes the surrounding seas of Japan one of the world's richest sources of fish, and its abundant seafood varies enormously from season to season and region to region.

Religion has also influenced Japan's culinary history. Buddhism spread through to the general public as early as the 8th century, and the Japanese were largely vegetarian and mainly ate what was available in the fields and mountains – with occasional fish from the rivers, lakes and seas – all cooked in abundantly available water. It wasn't until Japan opened up to the West in the late 19th century that the people started eating meat.

Many things, from Buddhism to *hashi* (chopsticks), even the origin of sushi, have been influenced by China. Numerous ingredients are common to both cuisines, but cooking methods are entirely different: Japanese cuisine tends to be water-based, and an entire meal can be made without a drop of oil. Many of the deep-fried and meat dishes in this book are relatively new to Japan, inspired by the cooking of China and other countries.

The *Easy Japanese Cookbook* shows you how to recreate this varied collection of simple, authentic dishes, from the classic miso soup to the gloriously colourful and invigorating sushi rolls. Each recipe is illustrated by a mouth-watering photograph and accompanied by easy-to-follow instructions, while the menu plans suggest ideas for every eating occasion, from a speedy light lunch to a sumptuous dinner party. The sections on ingredients, equipment and techniques provide practical information, helping you to make both traditional and contemporary Japanese recipes with ease and enjoyment.

PART 1

THE BASICS

*Japanese cooking is renowned for its **fresh**, subtle flavours, meticulous attention to detail and colourful, **creative** presentation. It is also surprisingly simple and easy. Although some of the **techniques** are quite different from other cuisines, you will soon **discover** that preparing Japanese food is an enjoyable and **fascinating** way to cook. The basic recipes in this opening chapter are at the heart of the cuisine and form the core of most meals. For example, an **authentic** Japanese meal would not be **complete** without plain boiled rice or sushi rice; then there is dashi, a key stock, as well as the **classic** accompaniments of **delicate** miso soup and flavoursome Japanese pickles.*

*Many once unfamiliar **ingredients**, from nori to shiitake mushrooms, and **essential** seasonings, such as shoyu, miso, rice vinegar and saké, are now readily available at **mainstream** supermarkets and oriental stores. These and many other **indispensable** items of the Japanese kitchen are detailed in the following pages.*

*Preparation is very **important** in Japanese cooking, and the key techniques are explained step by step. Once you **master** the basics, you will be well on your way to **successful** Japanese cooking. It's that simple and easy.*

INGREDIENTS

AZUKI

These nutritious, small red beans (also known as *adzuki*) are now widely available in supermarkets and health food shops in dried, canned and paste form. In Japan, they are most often used as a sweet paste for cakes and desserts known as *án*.

BAMBOO SHOOTS (TAKENOKO)

These are a popular vegetable in South-east Asia and are widely available ready-cooked in cans. However, the Japanese cherish the fresh young shoots, which are treated and valued as a seasonal delicacy. Bamboo shoots represent spring and are almost always simmered gently to protect their delicate flavour. The fresh shoots, cooked and vacuum-packed, are available at Japanese supermarkets. Use fresh bamboo shoots if you can find them, but canned ones will do if not.

BONITO (KATSUO)

Part of the same family as skipjack tuna, *katsuo*, known outside Japan as bonito, is one of the most important fish in Japanese cooking. It is cooked and dried whole to make *katsuo-bushi* (see dried bonito flakes, page 11), but the delicate flavour and meaty texture of fresh katsuo is best appreciated raw as sashimi. *Hatsu-gatsuo* (meaning "first katsuo"), caught at the beginning of the season (spring to early summer), is regarded as a delicacy. The autumn katsuo is known as *modori-gatsuo* ("returning katsuo"), as the fish return south. They are fatter, with a richer flavour and firmer texture.

CHINESE LEAVES OR CABBAGE (HAKUSAI)

Japanese *hakusai* (meaning "white vegetable") is larger and the outer leaves are in fact greener than the Western equivalent. Salt-pickled Chinese Leaves (see page 29) is one of the most popular dishes served to accompany plain cooked rice at the breakfast table. Chinese leaves are also used in simmered or steamed dishes and hotpots, or can be eaten raw in salads.

CURRY ROUX

This contains all the necessary ingredients, such as soup stock, spices and seasonings, for making a curry sauce, in a soft slab that resembles a bar of chocolate.

DAIKON

Daikon (meaning "big root") are long, white radishes, also known by the Indian name *mooli*. They are one of the most indispensable and versatile vegetables in Japanese cooking. They are added to soups and hotpots, chopped into salads, shredded to make a garnish for sashimi, or grated for use as a condiment for tempura, and so on. They are now widely available in oriental supermarkets.

DASHI

This Japanese stock made with dried fish, seaweed and various flavourings is used as a base for soups and stocks. There is a recipe for homemade *dashi* on page 27, but for small quantities use freeze-dried granules (*dashi-no-moto*).

DRIED AND PICKLED PLUMS (UMEBOSHI)

Umeboshi (meaning "dried plum") are Japanese apricots that are first sun-dried and then salted. It is a unique Japanese pickle, usually eaten with rice for breakfast. They are very salty, but are regarded as a tonic, aiding digestion and keeping the intestinal tract clear. They are often pickled with red shiso leaves for flavour as well as for their bright red colour. They are available from Japanese supermarkets.

DRIED BONITO FLAKES (HANA-GATSUO OR KEZURIBUSHI)

Katsuo (bonito or skipjack tuna) is cooked and dried whole into a hard block called katsuo-bushi and then shaved. The flake this produces is called hana-gatsuo (meaning "katsuo flower") or kezuribushi ("shaven block"). It is a vital ingredient in Dashi (see page 27) and it is also sprinkled over vegetables as a flavouring. It is available in packets at Japanese supermarkets.

DRIED MIXED SEA VEGETABLE SALAD (KAISO SALAD)

Mixed sea vegetable salad contains various beautiful green, red and white sea vegetables and is available in packets at Japanese supermarkets.

EDAMAME

Edamame (meaning "branch bean") are young green soya beans still in their pods. They are often sold on the stalk in Japan.

Elsewhere, they are normally sold cooked and frozen, either in or out of their pods, at good supermarkets and Japanese shops. Simply cook in salted boiling water and sprinkle with a little sea salt to eat. Eat them by taking a pod in your hand and squeezing it with your teeth to push the beans out.

ENOKI

Enoki, or enokitake, are bundles of tiny, berry-capped mushrooms with long, thin stems. The wild versions have a brownish orange cap and grow on the stumps of enoki, poplar and persimmon trees in winter, but cultivated versions grown at a low temperature, without light, produce the bundles of white caps that are found in supermarkets. Enoki are mainly used in hotpots in Japan, but are eaten raw in the West.

GINGER

Vinegar-pickled root ginger as an accompaniment to sushi is the most well-known ginger dish outside Japan, but for other Japanese cooking only the juice, squeezed from grated ginger, is used. Fresh ha-shoga (ginger shoot) and mé-shoga (ginger sprout) are available in summer in Japan. Fresh ginger shoot is also vinegar-pickled and used as a garnish for grilled fish dishes. To remove the skin, scrape using the edge of a teaspoon.

GINGKO NUT (GINNAN)

The Japanese maple tree, icho, bears the gingko nut, known as ginnan in Japanese. The word gingko, or ginkgo, is a corruption of *ginkyo*, another Japanese name for the tree. Fresh gingko nut in its shell is available only in autumn in Japan, but shelled and cooked nuts in cans, jars or vacuum-sealed packets are sold at oriental supermarkets. Crack open the shell of fresh nuts, peel the membrane and lightly grill, then eat sprinkled with a little salt. In cooking, they are often used as a garnish for their gorgeous yellow colour (fresh ones are green).

GYOZA WRAPPERS

Widely available at oriental supermarkets, these thin, round pancakes made of wheat flour are used to make a type of dumpling that originated in China. They are normally about 7.5cm/3in in diameter and come in packets of 24 sheets.

HARUSAME VERMICELLI

These very fine vermicelli are made from potatoes, sweet potatoes or green beans. Bought dried at oriental supermarkets, *harusame* need soaking for 5 minutes and then can be used in salads and soups. Cellophane noodles can be used instead.

KABOCHA SQUASH

Originally from Central America, this squash has a thick, dark green skin and glorious, orange-coloured flesh. With its dense texture and sweet, rich, nutty flavour, it is considered by some as the best among the squash family and is now obtainable at high-quality grocers and some supermarkets. *Kabocha* can be simply steamed or boiled, fried in tempura or

simmered with other ingredients in a hotpot. The seeds, dry-roasted in the shells, make a healthy, tasty snack.

KANTEN

Also known as agar-agar, *kanten* is the gum from tengursa, a red algae, and has been widely used in Japanese cooking since its discovery in Japan in the mid-17th century. The marine plant is dried in the sun, then boiled to extract the gum, which is then freeze-dried and made into blocks, strips, flakes or powder. It is a very efficient gelling agent and will set within 30 minutes at room temperature. Kanten makes a slightly opaque jelly that is easy to cut. It can be eaten as it is or used as a general thickener for soups and sauces.

KONBU

The giant dried *konbu*, also known as kombu or kelp, is one of the most indispensable ingredients in Japanese cooking and is vital in Dashi (see page 27). Dried konbu is also commercially processed to make numerous konbu by-products, such as cut konbu for savoury snacks and *tsukudani* (slow-simmered savouries). Also *tororo-konbu* (shaven konbu) is a thin, almost transparent sheet used for wrapping rice and snacks. Konbu and its by-products are available at oriental supermarkets.

KONNYAKU

Konnyaku is made from the starchy corm of the konnyaku plant (a kind of yam). It is typically a mottled grey colour and has a firm, jelly-like texture and mild seaweed-like flavour. This "yam cake" is bought in slabs. The Japanese love its unusual texture, but others may find it takes getting used to.

LOTUS ROOT (RENKON)

The several vertical holes running through this root create a flower-like pattern when it is cut into cross-sections, and it is for this unusual pattern that lotus root is most appreciated. Although its crunchy texture is very pleasant, the taste is not as impressive. Fresh lotus root is available at oriental supermarkets; Japanese supermarkets sell vacuum-packed ready-to-use lotus roots. Plunge peeled fresh lotus root into vinegared water to avoid discolouration, and do not use metal pans.

MATCHA

Matcha is a powdered green tea used mainly for tea ceremonies. The tea is made by whisking the powder in hot water in individual cups using a bamboo whisk, rather than brewing it in a pot. It is available in Japanese supermarkets.

MIRIN

This amber-coloured, heavily sweetened alcoholic liquid made from *shochu* (distilled saké) is used only in cooking. It adds a mild sweetness and a faint saké aroma as well as an attractive shiny glaze to dishes. Now used as a flavouring in European dishes, *mirin* is found not only at oriental shops but also at many supermarkets. But be aware: there is also a synthetically made, cheap mirin-like liquid available called *mirin-fumi* (mirin flavouring) as opposed to *hon-mirin* (real mirin). The alcohol content of hon mirin is 14 per cent, mirin fumi just 1 per cent.

MISO

This is one of the oldest and most important of Japanese flavourings. Boiled *daizu* (soya beans) are crushed, then mixed with a culture called *koji*, which is made with wheat and rice, barley or beans. The fermented mixture is allowed to mature for up to three years. Numerous types of *miso* are available at Japanese supermarkets, grouped into four basic grades according to colour and strength of flavour: *shiro* (white, light), *aka* (red, medium), *kuro* (black, strong) and standard (khaki, lighter than aka miso). Standard miso is available at many supermarkets, and some types are sold at Japanese supermarkets ready-mixed with dashi to use in miso soup.

MITSUBA

A popular Japanese herb, *mitsuba* (meaning "three leaves") is used mainly as a garnish for soups and simmered dishes. It has three light green leaves on top of long, thin stalks, which can be used to tie food. It is available at Japanese supermarkets.

NORI

Due to the popularity of sushi, *nori* has become a star ingredient in Japanese cooking and is now widely available at supermarkets and health food shops. The thin, black sheet of dried laver seaweed is rich in vegetable protein, vitamins and minerals, and is reputed to prevent anaemia, hair loss and fatigue. The sheets are usually used for sushi and garnishes, while mini sheets are used for wrapping rice; some are ready-toasted or seasoned. Nori is also used in other products such as *tsukudani* (slow-simmered savouries), nori-wrapped *senbei* (rice biscuit) and dried *aonori* (green nori flakes), which are sprinkled on rice.

PICKLED DAIKON (TAKUAN)

Renowned for being invented by the Buddhist monk Takuan in the 17th century, hence its name, this bright yellow daikon pickle is a morning delight on many Japanese breakfast tables. Just-harvested daikon is hung for two to three weeks, then salted and pickled in *nuka* (rice bran) for two to three months. Pickled daikon is an essential ingredient in rolled sushi.

PREPARED RICE BRAN

Rice bran mixed with salt and spices is sold in packets at Japanese supermarkets. It is used in rice bran pickles.

RAMEN

The word *ramen* comes from the Chinese *la-mien* (meaning "stretched noodle"), but the two are quite different in texture; ramen become slightly transparent when cooked and crunchier than Chinese egg noodles. In Japan, the popularity of ramen has long exceeded that of the more traditional udon and soba noodles, and ramen are now rapidly becoming popular in the West. They are available fresh, dried or frozen at oriental stores and large supermarkets. Instant ramen (dried ramen with soup and flavouring in a packet) are widely popular as a quick, healthy lunch, snack or late-night supper.

RICE (KOMÉ)

Komé, also called *o'komé*, is the most important staple food for the Japanese. The sacred grain is so important that the word for cooked rice, *gohan* or *meshi*, means "meal" itself. The short grain Japanese variety, as opposed to the neighbouring Asian countries' long grains, such as Thai fragrant and basmati, was developed over the centuries to suit the wet climate as well as the Japanese palate. There are over 300 different kinds of short grain rice grown all over Japan; among the most well known are *koshihikari* and *sasanishiki*, but those available outside Japan are mostly grown in California, although Spain also produces good Japanese rice. Japanese short grain rice is available at supermarkets and is often labelled as sushi rice. In addition to the ordinary white rice (*uruchimai*), brown rice (*génmai*) and glutinous rice (*mochigomé*) are also available.

RICE VINEGAR (SU)

Japanese vinegar, *su*, also called *o'su*, is made from rice and other grains, and it is milder, sweeter and less acidic than white wine vinegar. It is split into four grades by its rice content and priced accordingly: *junmai-su* (pure rice vinegar), *komesu* or *yonezu* (over 40g/1½oz of rice per litre/35fl oz/4 cups of vinegar), *kokumotsu-su* (grain vinegar; less than 40g/1½oz of rice per litre) and *gosei-su* (which contains synthetically made vinegar). They are all sold as rice vinegar at Japanese supermarkets, so you will need to check which grade you want. The Japanese rice vinegar sold at other oriental shops and local supermarkets is likely to be either gosei-su or kokumotsu-su. Rice vinegar has many qualities: it can be used to refresh vegetables and reduce saltiness, it has antibacterial qualities; and it acts as a coagulant for protein foods. It also prevents food from discolouring, helps to wash off slimy substances from foods and can even soften small fish bones. It is, therefore, useful in Japanese cookery from early preparation stage through to seasoning.

SAKÉ

Saké has played a vital role in the evolution of Japanese cuisine. Made from rice, the sacred grain, and consequently revered as a sacred liquid, the first brew is still dedicated to local Shinto temples each year. Although the Japanese drink less saké nowadays, nothing really matches its mellow, delicate flavour to accompany Japanese food. Saké is also frequently used in cooking to give a delicate flavour and unique, refreshing lightness to a dish. There are 55,000 different kinds of saké and 6,000 brands produced by about 2,000 brewers in Japan, ranging from mass-produced brands to smaller regional, more exclusive names. Whereas only very limited top-quality brands are available at Japanese supermarkets, factory-made ones such as Ozeki, Gekkeikan, Shochikubai, Takara Masamune

and Hakushika are widely available at quality stores. Cheap saké for cooking is also available at Japanese supermarkets.

SANSHO

Sansho (meaning "mountain pepper") is not as pungent as black pepper but its soothing, minty aroma adds a subtle acidic flavour to a dish. The sansho plant is used at every stage of its growth from spring through to autumn. The delicate young sprout, called *kinomé*, is used as a garnish for steamed dishes and soups. The tiny greenish yellow flowers, *hana-zansho*, that appear in spring, are used for garnishing sashimi, and the bitterly pungent berries, *mi-* or *tsubu-zansho*, in early summer are simmered and used with rice and soups. The most popular is *kona-zansho* (powdered sansho), which is made from the seed pods in autumn and used as a condiment. Both tsubu-zansho and kona-zansho are available at Japanese supermarkets.

SATOIMO

A kind of taro tuber, *satoimo* has a slightly sweet flavour and a rich, dense texture. Underneath the hairy, striped, dark skin there is a unique slipperiness, which makes the vegetable very easy to peel. It is eaten boiled or steamed, then dipped in shoyu, as a snack, as well as being simmered in dishes and soups.

SESAME SEEDS

Sesame plants grow in tropical and subtropical regions all over the world, and the seeds are used in many cuisines.

In Japanese cooking, sesame also plays an important role, and is normally available as seeds, both white and black, ground or in paste form. The seeds are normally roasted and are called *iri-goma* or *atari-goma*. To bring out their nutty aroma, rich flavour and crunchy texture, always lightly dry-fry over a medium heat, moving the seeds in the pan constantly, for up to 1 minute until they just turn golden. Half-crush the seeds using a mortar and pestle to bring out their flavour.

SEVEN-SPICE CHILLI POWDER (SHICHIMI)

Shichimi is widely available from oriental supermarkets and is made with powdered dried chilli mixed with other seeds, usually sesame, poppy, hemp, shiso and sansho, as well as nori. A dried powder made from chilli only, called *ichimi*, is also available. They are both used as condiments and sprinkled over soups, noodles, yakitori and grilled foods.

SHIITAKE

These brown-capped mushrooms grow under trees such as the *shii* (*Pasania cuspidata*), oak and chestnut, though today they are cultivated on a huge scale. Dried shiitake have a much stronger flavour, but fresh shiitake tend to be used in Japanese cooking for their subtlety. To prepare fresh shiitake, wipe off any earth and dirt with a damp piece of kitchen paper and trim off the hard part of the stem before cooking. Shiitake are one of the regular ingredients in hotpot dishes and tempura, and can also be simply barbecued. Soak dried shiitake in cold water for about 1 hour or, if you are in a hurry, soak in warm water for 30 minutes before use. Both fresh and dried forms are widely available.

SHIMEJI

Shimeji are Japanese mushrooms with a small button-like cap and about a 7.5cm/3in long stem. They grow in the autumn in bunches or in circles under trees such as *nara* (Japanese oak) and red pine, but they are also cultivated. They have little aroma and a delicate flavour, but are valued for their fresh, meaty texture, which suits delicate Japanese dishes. Trim off the spongy, bottom part and quickly rinse under cold water. Using your fingers, separate the stems and cook lightly. Shimeji are available at quality grocers and supermarkets.

SHIRATAKI

Shirataki (meaning "white waterfall") are thin white noodle-like filaments of shredded konnyaku. These "yam noodles" are sold fresh in inflated plastic bags filled with water or in cans in Japanese supermarkets. They are mainly used for hotpots and salads.

SHISO

Also known as *ohba* in Japan, *shiso* is the most popularly used herb in Japanese cooking. A member of the mint family, it has a wide, diamond-shaped leaf, about 10cm/4in long and 7.5cm/3in wide. The green form is used for its exquisite flavour and the red for its colour and aroma. The whole plant is used as a herb or garnish mostly for sushi and sashimi dishes. The green leaves are sold year round in packets at Japanese supermarkets.

SHOYU

Known as soy sauce in the West, *shoyu* is no doubt the single most important ingredient in Japanese cooking and is used in many recipes. It derives from Japan's ancient seasoning called *hishio*, which was fermented with grains such as rice and wheat or soya beans, and the exuded liquid became shoyu. Today, it is mass produced and has become one of the most popular flavourings all over the world. There are various grades, such as *usukuchi* (light) and *koikuchi* (dark), but the difference is small. The richest in flavour, *tamari*, is made purely from soya beans. Shoyu should be used for all relevant recipes in this book.

SOBA

Soba are uniquely Japanese noodles made of buckwheat flour usually mixed with ordinary wheat flour. They are firmer than wheat noodles, have a crunchy texture and are good for the health. They range from dark brownish grey to light beige, depending on how the buckwheat is ground. Green soba noodles, called *cha-soba*, contain matcha.

SOMEN

These fine wheat noodles are produced in much the same way as *udon* (see page 18). With the help of vegetable oil, the dough is stretched to make very thin strips, which are then air-dried and are so fine that they take only 1 minute to cook.

SOYA BEANS (DAIZU)

Daizu (meaning "big beans") feature prominently in Japanese cooking. Their use as whole beans is, however, limited to simple dishes such as Simmered Soya Beans (see page 146), but they are the base of many ingredients, such as shoyu (soy sauce), miso, tofu and *kinako* (daizu flour), and are used for *wagashi* (Japanese cakes) and other sweet snacks. When fermented, they become *natto* — a popular breakfast food.

THIN DEEP-FRIED TOFU (ABURA-AGE)

This form of tofu normally comes in standard-size sheets 13 x 6 x 1cm thick/5 x 2½ x ½in, and is one of the popular additions to miso soup. It can also be split open like pitta bread and stuffed with sushi rice to make Inari-zushi (see page 92) and is available, often frozen, at Japanese supermarkets.

TOFU

To make tofu, soya beans are first boiled and crushed, then the milk is separated and made into curds with the help of a coagulant. The set curds are then scooped into a cloth-lined wooden mould and pressed for a few hours to allow the excess water to drain away and for the tofu to firm up. This tofu often has a distinctive cloth mark on its sides and is known as *momen-goshi* (meaning "cotton-sieved") or firm tofu in the West.

By contrast, silken *kinu-goshi* ("silk-sieved") tofu, which can be soft or firm, is set directly in the mould without being drained.

TONKATSU SAUCE

This sauce, which contains fruits, vegetables, spices and shoyu, is available in bottles at Japanese supermarkets

TUNA

Known as *maguro* in Japan, tuna is a large member of the mackerel family. There are several kinds used in Japan: blue-fin, big-eye, yellow-fin, long-finned and southern blue-fin. For sashimi and sushi, blue-fin is normally used. The red meat from the main, upper part of the body is called *akami* (red flesh) as opposed to *toro* (oily meat) from the lower body. Toro is classified by the degree of oiliness: *chu-toro* (medium toro) or *o-toro* (big toro). At Japanese supermarkets, tuna is normally sold in thick rectangular pieces for sushi and sashimi.

UDON

These thick noodles are popular all over the world. They are made from a wheat flour and salted water dough, which is rolled out and thinly sliced. Dried *udon* are widely available, and cooked and frozen udon are available in oriental supermarkets.

WAKAME

Wakame (meaning "young sprouts") is a brownish orange algae that is full of vitamins and has absolutely no fat. A popular addition to miso soup, wakame is also delicious served as a salad with a vinegary dressing. For culinary use, it is mostly dried or salted. The most commonly used types are packets of cut wakame, which soften almost instantly. To use in salads, soak the wakame in plenty of water for about 5 minutes, drain and pour boiling water over, then plunge into cold water. Some do not need pre-soaking and can be put straight into soups.

WASABI

Wasabi (mountain hollyhock) is said to have antiseptic qualities and is an indispensable accompaniment to sushi and sashimi. In Japan, freshly grated wasabi is often served, but elsewhere it is available either in paste or powdered form. Both forms tend to contain horseradish to give it an extra kick. To make a paste, put 1 heaped teaspoon powdered wasabi in an egg cup and add the same volume of tepid water. Stir vigorously to make a clay-like paste. Place the cup upside down on a board to stand for at least 10 minutes before use.

WOOD EAR FUNGUS (KIKURAGE)

Literally translated as "tree jellyfish" but known as "wood ear" in China, *kikurage* are black, ear-shaped fungi grown on dead trees such as mulberry and elm. They are normally available dried in packets at oriental supermarkets and need to be soaked in warm water for 10–15 minutes before use. Unlike other mushrooms, they are crunchy in texture and are mainly used in simmered dishes and vinegary salads.

TECHNIQUES

SLICING FISH FILLETS

Ask your fishmonger to gut and fillet the fish for you. Remove any bones using tweezers. Once you have skinned the fish (see right), you are ready to slice it.

For sushi and sashimi, slice a fish fillet crossways by placing it on a cutting board, then insert the blade of a very sharp knife at a slight angle and cut downwards into 1cm/½in thick slices.

Buy larger fish, such as tuna and salmon, for sushi and sashimi as a chunk, rather than steaks, and first cut it into blocks approximately 7.5cm wide x 2.5cm thick/3 x 1in before slicing similarly into slices 7.5cm long x 1cm thick/3 x ½in.

For nigiri (hand-moulded) sushi, slice a fish fillet (sea bass, mackerel, etc.) crossways so that the cut side measures about 7.5cm/3in long. Insert the blade of a very sharp knife at a slight angle and cut downwards into pieces approximately 7.5cm long x 4cm wide x 0.5cm thick/3 x 1½ x ¼in. Each piece should be able to cover the top and sides of a hand-moulded log of sushi rice, about the size of a slightly fat thumb.

Buy larger fish, such as tuna and salmon, for nigiri as a chunk, rather than steaks, and cut it into blocks approximately 7.5cm wide x 2.5cm thick/3 x 1in of any length before slicing similarly into pieces approximately 7.5cm long x 4cm wide x 0.5cm thick/3 x 1½ x ¼in.

SKINNING FISH

Always skin fillets, except mackerel. With mackerel, remove only the thin outer membrane, leaving the silver pattern intact.

1 PLACE a fillet skin-side down on a cutting board and, gripping the skin firmly at the tail end with one hand, insert the blade of a very sharp knife at a slight angle between the skin and flesh.
2 SLIDE the blade between the skin and the flesh towards the head to remove the skin.

HANDLING PRAWNS

Prawns are used frequently in Japanese cooking, particularly in tempura, sushi and sashimi. Ideally, use fresh raw prawns still in their shells.

To devein:
1 REMOVE the head from the prawn with your fingers and insert a cocktail stick, from the side, through the first gap in the shell from the head.
2 PICK up the vein with the cocktail stick and, using your fingers, very gently pull the rest of the vein out.

To keep prawns straight while cooking:
1 INSERT a cocktail stick lengthways into the prawn through the body, straightening it, and cook with the stick in.
2 REMOVE the cocktail stick carefully when the prawn is cooked and has cooled a little but is not yet cold.

PICKLED RADISH FLOWERS

These decorative radish flowers make an attractive addition and are surprisingly easy to make. After cutting, the radishes are steeped in a Japanese rice vinegar marinade, which helps to keep the vegetables fresh, open out the "petals" and prevent discolouration.

1 TRIM the bottom of a radish to make a flat base. Lay 2 pencils, side-by-side, on a cutting board and place a radish upright in between. Using a sharp knife, carefully make 4–6 vertical cuts in the radish until the blade touches the pencils, so that the radish is not cut through to the bottom.

2 TURN the radish 90 degrees and make a few more cuts across the cuts already made to make a criss-cross pattern. Repeat to make as many radish flowers as desired.

3 PUT the radishes in a mixing bowl, sprinkle lightly with salt and lightly rub in. Leave for 10 minutes.

4 MIX together 150ml/5fl oz/scant ⅔ cup rice vinegar and 85g/3oz/scant ½ cup sugar, stirring until the sugar dissolves. Drain the radishes, gently squeeze out the excess water and pour the vinegar mixture over them. Leave to marinate for 2–3 hours or refrigerate overnight, during which time they open out a little to resemble "cherry blossoms".

5 SIEVE some hard-boiled egg yolks to form yellow crumbs, and place these on some of the radish flowers as "pollen".

VARIATIONS

DAIKON CHRYSANTHEMUM – Cut a peeled daikon into 2.5–4cm/1–1½in thick rounds and make deep criss-cross cuts about three-quarters of the way through each slice. Quarter each round, then follow steps 3 and 4 for the radish flowers, marinating the daikon for 4–6 hours or leaving it refrigerated overnight. Serve topped with thinly sliced dried red chilli rings.

TURNIP FLOWERS – Follow steps 1 and 2 for the radish flowers, using small peeled turnips, making 8–12 cuts in each one, then follow steps 3 and 4, marinating the turnips for 4–6 hours or leaving them refrigerated overnight. Place a thinly sliced dried chilli ring on top as "pollen", if wanted.

PICKLED LOTUS ROOT FLOWERS

In Japan, lotus root is greatly appreciated for its shape, which looks similar to a flower when thinly sliced crossways.

1 PREPARE the pickle marinade for the lotus root flower by mixing together 5 tbsp rice vinegar, 5 tbsp mirin and a pinch of salt in a saucepan, then bring to the boil over a medium heat for a few seconds. Meanwhile, soak 1 dried red chilli in hot water for 5 minutes.

2 REMOVE the pan from the heat. Drain the red chilli, then cut it into thin rings, discard the seeds and add to the marinade. Leave the marinade to cool.

3 PEEL the fresh lotus root and plunge into 250ml/9fl oz/ 1 cup water mixed with 2 tbsp vinegar to prevent it discolouring. Remove the lotus root and pat dry.

4 HOLD the lotus root vertically in your hand and, using a sharp knife, make 2 vertical incisions, about 1cm/½in deep, to make a V-shaped channel between 2 of the large holes. (Lotus root normally has 7 regularly spaced, large holes running through the root in a circle, with several little circles dotted around.) Repeat these cuts 6 more times.

5 SLICE crossways into thin "flower-shapes". Put them in the marinade and leave to marinate for 1 hour, or overnight. Take lotus flowers out of the marinade as you need them.

MAKING CARROT FLOWERS

These simple flowers make a wonderful addition, as their bright colour catches the eye (see page 133).

1 USE a sharp knife to make 5 small V-shaped slits at equal intervals lengthways on the carrot skin.

2 SMOOTH out the cut edges to make 5 petal shapes when the carrot is viewed from the top.

3 SLICE off about 0.5cm/¼in from the top end of the carrot diagonally towards the centre (like sharpening a pencil) and slice off a very thin piece. Continue slicing to make as many flowers as desired.

CUTTING VEGETABLES

In Japanese cooking, the accurate and precise cutting of ingredients is very important. Vegetables are normally cut into a similar shape and size for a dish to get them all cooked evenly.

For thin shreds, peel the vegetable stated in the recipe, then cut crossways into 5cm/2in long pieces. Thinly cut each piece lengthways, then slice again to make thin shreds.

For matchsticks, peel the vegetable stated in the recipe, then cut lengthways into thin slices. Stack a few slices together and cut them lengthways into thin pieces resembling matchsticks.

SLICING MEAT

It is usual for meat to be sliced very thinly in Japanese cooking, especially for dishes like Sukiyaki (see page 106). To make slicing easier, buy a chunk of meat rather than a steak.

1 FREEZE the meat for 3–4 hours. Remove the meat from the freezer and leave to half-thaw; it can take 1–2 hours at room temperature or 2–3 hours in the fridge. The half-frozen meat should still be firm enough to hold its shape.

2 HOLD a very sharp knife at a slight angle to the meat and cut it downwards into slices of the required thickness. Spread the slices on a plate to thaw thoroughly before use.

EQUIPMENT

BAMBOO SKEWERS

The most useful size is a thin skewer, about 15cm/6in long, which is used for grilling food such as Grilled Skewered Chicken (see page 38). Soak the skewers in water for at least 30 minutes before use to prevent them burning while grilling. Shorter, more elaborate skewers are used for serving

BAMBOO SUSHI MAT (MAKISU)

This bamboo mat, about the size of a table mat, is useful for rolling sushi into a cylinder.

CHOPSTICKS

A pair of *hashi* (chopsticks) are the most useful tools to cook with as well as the most elegant cutlery to eat with. There are various types and sizes for eating, cooking and serving.

GRATERS

A Japanese grater allows any juices from grated daikon or ginger to be captured in the curved base or the box below. There is one size for grating daikon and a half-sized version for root ginger and fresh wasabi. The latter is most useful

GRINDER AND PESTLE

The Japanese *suribachi* and *surikogi* (grinder and wooden pestle) grinds finer granules or pastes than a Western mortar and pestle and is ideal for small items such as sesame seeds. A small electric grinder makes a good alternative.

KNIVES

Since accurate and efficient cutting is so important in Japanese cooking, good Japanese knives are a cook's most cherished utensils. It is essential to have a good, sharp all-purpose knife and a small vegetable knife.

MOULDS

There are various shapes and sizes of moulds available, but a wooden mould for sushi and a metal one for all other set foods, such as jellies, should suffice.

RICE COOKER

A rice cooker cooks perfect, fluffy rice every time and keeps it warm until needed. It normally slow-cooks the rice, so cooking takes longer than it would in a saucepan over a direct heat, but you don't need to soak the rice first, which saves time. You can buy wonderful rice cookers that can recreate the taste of wood-fire cooked rice of olden days as closely as possible.

SUSHI TUB

A wooden sushi tub (*handai* or *hangiri* in Japanese) is a useful tool if you make sushi regularly. It is used to mix the cooked rice with the vinegar mixture and is usually made of Japanese cypress wood, which has the right porosity to absorb any excess moisture. If you cannot find a sushi tub, a large mixing bowl is an acceptable substitute.

BASIC RECIPES

PLAIN BOILED JAPANESE RICE
GOHAN

SERVES 4 PREPARATION TIME: 5 MINUTES, PLUS 40 MINUTES STANDING
COOKING TIME: 15 MINUTES

Japanese cooking begins with preparing rice. Cook it with care and patience and it will feel soothingly soft, yet gorgeously weighty, once in the mouth.

1 WASH 250g/9oz/scant 1¼ cups Japanese short grain rice thoroughly in several changes of water until the water runs clear, to remove the starch. Drain the rice in a strainer.

2 PUT the rice in a heavy-based, ideally cast-iron, saucepan, approximately 14cm/5½in in diameter. Add 300ml/10½fl oz/ scant 1¼ cups water and leave for 30 minutes.

3 COVER the saucepan with a lid and bring to the boil over a medium heat. Lower the heat to minimum and, using a wooden spatula, quickly stir the rice from top to bottom. Replace the lid and simmer slowly over a very low heat for 10–12 minutes until the water has been absorbed but bubbles are still forming on top of the rice.

4 TURN the rice gently from bottom to top with the spatula. Continue to simmer, covered, for another minute. Remove from the heat and leave to stand, covered, for 10 minutes. The rice is ready to be served in individual rice bowls, or shaped with wet hands into small "logs", 4 x 5cm/1½ x 2in, for bento boxes.

SUSHI RICE
SUMESHI

SERVES 4 PREPARATION TIME: 10 MINUTES
COOKING TIME: 15 MINUTES

The most important part of sushi making is to get the rice right. Be aware of the 3Ts: texture, temperature and tenderness. If you get these correct, you are almost there.

250g/9oz/scant 1¼ cups **Japanese short grain rice**
3 tbsp **rice vinegar**
1 tbsp **sugar**
1 tsp **sea salt**

1 PREPARE and cook the rice following the method for Plain Boiled Japanese Rice (*see left*).

2 MIX the vinegar, sugar and salt in a cup and stir well until dissolved.

3 TRANSFER the hot rice to a non-metallic mixing bowl and sprinkle the vinegar dressing over it. Using a wooden spatula, fold the vinegar mixture into the rice – do not stir. Quickly cool the rice using a fan while gently turning it with the spatula.

4 LEAVE the rice to cool to lukewarm before using it to make sushi.

RICE COOKED WITH PEAS
AOMAME GOHAN

SERVES 4   PREPARATION TIME: 10 MINUTES, PLUS 40 MINUTES
STANDING   COOKING TIME: 15 MINUTES

The subtle aroma and flavour of the peas give Japanese rice another dimension with a striking contrast in colour – a great spring-summer dish.

250g/9oz/scant 1¼ cups **Japanese short grain rice**

1 tbsp **saké**

¾ tsp **sea salt**

60g/2oz/⅓ cup frozen **peas** or petits pois

1 WASH the rice thoroughly in several changes of water until the water runs clear. Drain the rice in a strainer.

2 PUT the rice in a heavy-based, ideally cast-iron, saucepan, approximately 14cm/5½in in diameter. Add 300ml/10½fl oz/ scant 1¼ cups water and leave for 30 minutes.

3 MIX in the saké and salt and top with the peas or petits pois. Cover the saucepan and bring to the boil over a medium heat. Lower the heat to minimum and, using a wooden spatula, quickly stir the rice from top to bottom. Replace the lid and simmer for 10–12 minutes until the water has been absorbed but bubbles are still forming on top of the rice.

4 TURN the rice gently from bottom to top, then continue to simmer, covered, for 1 minute. Remove from the heat and leave to stand, covered, for 10 minutes. Lightly mix the rice so that the peas are evenly spread, then serve hot in bowls.

RICE COOKED WITH SHIMEJI
SHIMEJI GOHAN

SERVES 4   PREPARATION TIME: 10 MINUTES, PLUS 10 MINUTES
STANDING   COOKING TIME: 15 MINUTES

The meaty texture of the Japanese shimeji mushroom, coupled with its pretty shape, gives bite and richness to plain rice.

250g/9oz/scant 1¼ cups **Japanese short grain rice**

300ml/10½fl oz/scant 1¼ cups **Dashi** (*see page 27*), left to cool

1 tbsp **saké**

½ tsp **sea salt**

1½ tsp **shoyu**

60g/2oz **shimeji mushrooms**, trimmed and separated into individual stems

1 tbsp finely chopped **chives**

1 PREPARE the rice following the method for Rice Cooked with Peas (*see left*), but use dashi instead of water in step 2, add the shoyu with the saké and salt in step 3 and use shimeji instead of peas.

2 SPRINKLE the cooked rice with chives before serving.

DASHI
DASHI

MAKES 1 LITRE/35FL OZ/4 CUPS PREPARATION TIME: 5 MINUTES, PLUS 1 HOUR SOAKING COOKING TIME: 10 MINUTES

Dashi, the basic Japanese stock, is used not only for soups but also for almost all simmering dishes and sauces. It's very easy to make authentic dashi and it can be frozen for later use.

15–20cm/6–8in piece dried **konbu**

30g/1oz dried **bonito flakes**

1 WIPE the konbu with damp kitchen paper, put it in a saucepan with 1.25 litres/44fl oz/5 cups water and leave to soak for 1 hour.

2 BRING the water with the konbu to the boil, removing the konbu just before the water reaches boiling point to retain its subtle flavour. (The konbu can be discarded at this point or reserved for future use.)

3 REDUCE the heat to low and add the dried bonito flakes to the pan, then simmer for 5 minutes (do not allow the water to boil). Remove the pan from the heat and leave the stock to stand for a few minutes until the fish flakes settle to the bottom of the pan.

4 STRAIN the liquid through a sieve lined with muslin or kitchen paper. Discard the fish flakes. The stock is now ready to use.

MISO SOUP WITH WAKAME AND TOFU
WAKAME TO TOFU NO MISO SHIRU

SERVES 4 PREPARATION TIME: 10 MINUTES COOKING TIME: 10 MINUTES

Miso is used daily in one way or the other in the Japanese household, but is most commonly used as a base for soup. You can use a combination of any vegetables, tofu, seafood or even meat for the soup, but tofu coupled with wakame is the most traditional and popular choice.

5g/⅛oz dried **wakame**

600ml/21fl oz/scant 2½ cups **Dashi** *(see left)*

2–3 tbsp **khaki miso**

½ block **soft tofu**, about 150g/5½oz, cut into small cubes

1 **spring onion**, finely chopped

1 SOAK the dried wakame in plenty of warm water for 5 minutes, then drain. If the wakame is not already cut, chop it into small bite-sized pieces.

2 PUT the dashi in a saucepan and warm over a medium heat; do not allow it to boil. Put the miso in a cup and dilute it with some of the hot dashi from the pan. Pour three-quarters of this mixture into the pan. Taste and gradually add the remaining diluted miso, to taste.

3 ADD the wakame and tofu and heat over a medium heat. Just before it boils, remove the pan from the heat. Serve in soup bowls, sprinkled with the chopped spring onion.

CLEAR SOUP WITH BEATEN EGG
TAMAGO NO SUMASHI JIRU

SERVES 4   PREPARATION TIME: 10 MINUTES
COOKING TIME: 15 MINUTES

This is a Japanese-style consommé, the essence of which lies in the soup base rather than the added extras. A proper home-made dashi is best.

5cm/2in piece **daikon**, peeled and sliced lengthways into
   5cm/2in strips

20g/¾oz **mangetout**, trimmed

600ml/21fl oz/scant 2½ cups **Dashi** *(see page 27)*

¾ tsp **sea salt**

1 tbsp **shoyu**

2 **eggs**, beaten

1 **PUT** the daikon in a saucepan, cover with water and bring to the boil, then reduce the heat and simmer for 4–5 minutes until tender but still crunchy. Drain.

2 **COOK** the mangetout in the same way for 1–2 minutes. Drain and place under cold running water to cool quickly.

3 **HEAT** the dashi over a medium heat and mix in the salt and shoyu. Add the beaten eggs and, when the eggs float to the surface, gently stir with chopsticks (see page 23) or a fork to separate. Remove from the heat just before boiling.

4 **DIVIDE** the daikon between 4 soup bowls and pour the soup over. Serve immediately with the mangetout.

VINEGAR-PICKLED GINGER
AMAZU SHOGA

SERVES 4   PREPARATION TIME: 15 MINUTES, PLUS 3–4 DAYS PICKLING
COOKING TIME: 4 MINUTES

Otherwise known as gari *in sushi-shop jargon, vinegar-pickled ginger is an indispensable accompaniment to sushi. It is delicious to eat and also works as a mouth freshener in between sushi dishes. A variation, kine-shoga, is fresh ginger pickled in vinegar water, and this is popularly used to accompany grilled fish.*

100g/3½oz **root ginger**

VINEGAR MARINADE:

100ml/3½fl oz/scant ½ cup **rice vinegar**

1½ tbsp **sugar**

1 **PEEL** the ginger, then slice very thinly using a vegetable peeler. Put the ginger in a saucepan, cover with water and bring to the boil. Cook for 2 minutes, then drain.

2 **PUT** the rice vinegar, sugar and 3 tbsp water in a mixing bowl and stir until the sugar has dissolved.

3 **SQUEEZE** out the excess water from the ginger, then add the ginger to the vinegar marinade. Leave to pickle for 3–4 days, then store in an airtight container in the fridge for up to 12 months.

4 **SERVE** several slices folded like a flower or piled on a plate along with sushi or in a small separate dish.

SALT-PICKLED CHINESE LEAVES

HAKUSAI NO SHIOZUKE

SERVES 4–8   PREPARATION TIME: 20 MINUTES,
PLUS 12 HOURS PICKLING

*Rice and pickles go hand-in-hand at a Japanese table and there are
numerous methods of pickling all sorts of vegetables along with regional
varieties. This simple salt pickle is the most popular.*

10 **Chinese leaves**, halved lengthways, then cut into

   5cm/2in long pieces

juice of ½ **lime**, plus rind cut into 8 strips

2 **dried red chillies**

2 x 5cm/2in square pieces dried **konbu**

2 tbsp **sea salt**

1 **PUT** the white part of the Chinese leaves in a large mixing
bowl and top with half of the lime rind, 1 chilli and 1 piece
of konbu. Add the rest of the Chinese leaves and top with
the remaining lime rind, chilli and konbu.

2 **MIX** 100ml/3½oz/scant ½ cup water with the salt in a cup.
Stir until the salt dissolves, then add the lime juice. Pour
the mixture evenly over the Chinese leaves and place a flat
plate on top. The plate should be 2.5cm/1in smaller than the
diameter of the bowl so that it sits directly on top of the

Chinese leaves. Place a weight (about 1kg/2lb 4oz) on
top of the plate and leave to pickle for 12 hours until
the leaves have wilted.

3 **TURN** the Chinese leaves from top to bottom every few
hours so that the flavours of the konbu, chilli and lime rind
are evenly spread. (It will be ready to serve after 12 hours,
but can be kept in the fridge for up to 2 days.)

4 **REMOVE** the weight and plate. Drain the leaves and
remove the konbu, chilli and lime rind. Finely shred the
konbu, slice the chilli into rings and discard the lime rind.

5 **SQUEEZE** out the excess water from the Chinese leaves
and put them in a mixing bowl. Mix in the konbu and serve
the dish with the chilli rings.

VARIATION

FREEZER-BAG PICKLING – Cut as many Chinese leaves as
you like into about 5cm/2in square pieces. Put a handful in a
freezer bag and sprinkle with about ½ tsp sea salt. Add another
handful of leaves on top and sprinkle with another ½ tsp salt.
Repeat this process until all the leaves are in the bag. Squeeze
all the air out of the bag and seal tightly with a rubber band.
Put the bag in the fridge for 2–3 days, turning it around
occasionally so that the leaves wilt evenly. Take out the leaves,
drain them and squeeze out the excess water. Eat them with a
little shoyu or use in a salad.

MISO PICKLES
MISO-ZUKE

SERVES **4** PREPARATION TIME: **20** MINUTES, PLUS **3** HOURS PICKLING

Undiluted miso is very salty and can pickle vegetables within a few hours so they remain crunchy and fresh, unlike other wilted pickles.

2 small **carrots**, peeled

10cm/4in piece **daikon**, peeled and halved lengthways

1 **celery** stick, halved crossways

MISO MARINADE:

300g/10½oz **khaki miso**

2 tbsp **saké**

2 tbsp **mirin**

1 **MAKE** the miso marinade by mixing together the miso, saké and mirin in a bowl until smooth.

2 **PUT** half of the marinade in a non-metallic, shallow, rectangular dish and spread evenly. Put the carrots, daikon and celery on top in an even layer. Spoon the remaining marinade over the vegetables, cover with a lid or cling film and leave to marinate in the fridge. They will be ready to serve after 3 hours, but will keep crisp for up to 5 hours.

3 **REMOVE** the vegetables and rinse them under cold running water. Pat dry with kitchen paper, then slice into bite-sized pieces. Arrange on a plate and serve with rice. (Store the marinade in the fridge for another time.)

RICE BRAN PICKLES
NUKA-ZUKE

SERVES **4** PREPARATION TIME: **30** MINUTES, PLUS **12** HOURS PICKLING

Nuka (rice bran) mixed with strong brine is called nuka-miso. *It forms a rice bran bed that needs turning every day – a method of pickling unique to Japan. Rice bran and prepared rice bran are available at Japanese supermarkets.*

500g/1lb 2oz/3½ cups **prepared rice bran**

150g/5½oz/scant ¾ cup **sea salt**

1 **carrot**, peeled

5cm/2in piece **daikon**, peeled

10cm/4in piece **cucumber**

1 **PUT** the prepared rice bran in a large mixing bowl. Mix the salt with 400ml/14fl oz/scant 1⅔ cups water and stir until dissolved. Add the salty water to the rice bran and mix well with a wooden spatula to make a smooth rice bran bed.

2 **TRANSFER** to a large, non-metallic container with an airtight lid and leave, covered, for 5 days, turning twice a day.

3 **BURY** the carrot, daikon and cucumber deep in the rice bran and leave to pickle overnight. The pickles are ready to serve after 12 hours, but after 24 hours they become sour.

4 **REMOVE** the vegetables from the bran and rinse under cold running water. Pat dry and slice into bite-sized pieces.

5 **USE** the bran bed to pickle more vegetables, covering it with a layer of salt and storing it in the fridge when not in use. Add fresh bran now and then, and it will keep for ever.

JAPANESE THICK OMELETTE

TAMAGO-YAKI

MAKES 1 THICK ROLL   PREPARATION TIME: 5 MINUTES
COOKING TIME: 20 MINUTES

Thick-rolled omelette – layers of egg sheet rolled into one – is regularly eaten for breakfast in Japan and makes a useful addition to lunchboxes and sushi. The thin egg sheet variation has just one layer of egg, rather than four, and is used for sushi – thinly shredded for sprinkling as well as for wrapping.

3 tbsp **Dashi** *(see page 27)*

1½ tbsp **sugar**

1 tsp **shoyu**, plus extra to serve

a pinch **sea salt**

4 large **eggs**, beaten

2 tbsp **vegetable oil**

grated **daikon**, to serve

1 **MIX** together the dashi, sugar, shoyu, salt and beaten eggs and stir until the sugar dissolves.

2 **HEAT** a square *tamago-yaki* pan, or a non-stick frying pan about 14cm/5½in in diameter, over a medium heat and pour in the oil. Using kitchen paper, wipe off the excess oil and retain the oiled kitchen paper. Lower the heat.

3 **POUR** a quarter of the egg mixture into the pan to form an even layer. Prick any air bubbles with a fork.

4 **ROLL** up the thin egg sheet just before it completely sets and place the roll to one side of the pan. Oil the empty part of the pan, using the kitchen paper, and push the rolled egg to the oiled side, then oil the remainder of the pan. Pour in another quarter of the egg, which will form a thin egg sheet attached on one side to the roll. Roll up this new egg sheet using the first roll as its core. Repeat this oiling and rolling twice more.

5 **REMOVE** the omelette from the pan and cut into the required shape and size. Serve hot or cold, topped with the daikon and sprinkled with extra shoyu.

VARIATION

THIN EGG SHEET – Heat a square *tamago-yaki* pan, or a non-stick frying pan about 20cm/8in in diameter, and wipe with a little oil. Lower the heat, then pour in a beaten egg mixed with a pinch of salt and spread in a thin layer by tilting the pan. Cook for 30 seconds or until just set, then turn it over carefully. Remove the pan from the heat and leave the egg to stand for a few seconds, then turn out flat onto a cutting board to cool.

PART 2

THE RECIPES

The growing popularity of sushi, with its **exquisite** presentation and numerous health qualities, may have first **enticed** you to try Japanese food, but sushi is as fun to make as it is to eat. It is an **art** that may need a little practice, but I am certain you will enjoy the process and eating each **delicious** result nevertheless.

    Wonderful as it is, there is much more to Japanese cooking than just sushi, and the true diversity of this **fascinating** cuisine is depicted in this book, from the classic **favourites** such as Yakitori, Teriyaki and Tempura, to the less-familiar Japanese Beef Curry, Salmon Hotpot, Asparagus Chicken Rolls, Fried **Ramen** with Mixed Seafood and Rice Balls Wrapped in Sweet **Azuki** Paste.

    A **traditional** Japanese meal has many components and may start with Squash Miso Soup with Tofu and Mangetout, and **classics** such as this are truly **easy** dishes for cooks unfamiliar with Japanese cooking. Then you may like to go on to make a **starter** such as Seared Beef Tataki or opt for Assorted Sashimi, followed by **gorgeous** Sukiyaki or Monkfish Shabu-shabu. Desserts include the popular Half Gong Pancakes, **fragrant** Ginger Pears in Hot Plum Sauce and **stunning** Dragon Fruit with Cranberry Kanten.

SEARED BEEF TATAKI *GYUNIKU NO TATAKI*

**SERVES 4   PREPARATION TIME: 15 MINUTES, PLUS 3 HOURS MARINATING
COOKING TIME: 3 MINUTES**

*This is beef sashimi with a twist: the exterior is lightly seared but the inside is left
raw, then marinated in a wine sauce for 3 hours. This makes a substantial party
dish, particularly good for a hot summer's day with cold beer or wine.*

400g/14oz **beef fillet steak**

2 tbsp **vegetable oil**

12 **asparagus** spears, trimmed into 5cm/2in
pieces and par-boiled

sea salt and freshly ground **black pepper**

WINE MARINADE:

½ **onion**, thinly sliced into half-moons

½ **lime**, cut into half-moons

1 **garlic** clove, thinly sliced

150ml/5fl oz/scant ⅔ cup **white wine**

6 tbsp **shoyu**

DAIKON VINEGAR SAUCE:

3cm/1¼in piece **daikon**, peeled and grated

3 tbsp **shoyu**

3 tbsp **rice vinegar**

2 tbsp **mirin**

1 **SEASON** the beef with salt and pepper, rubbing it into the steak. Heat
the vegetable oil in a frying pan, then fry the steak, turning occasionally,
for 2–3 minutes until sealed and browned all over. Do not overcook —
the beef should be rare inside. Immediately plunge the beef into a bowl
of ice-cold water and rub off any burnt parts in the water. Drain and pat
dry with kitchen paper.

2 **MAKE** the wine marinade by mixing together the onion, lime, garlic,
wine and shoyu in a shallow, non-metallic bowl. Add the beef and leave
to marinate for 3 hours in the fridge, occasionally spooning the
marinade over. After 2 hours, add the asparagus spears to the marinade.

3 **DRAIN** the beef and asparagus spears and, using a very sharp knife,
slice the beef across the grain as thinly as you can.

4 **MAKE** the daikon vinegar sauce by putting the daikon, shoyu, rice
vinegar and mirin in a bowl and mixing well.

5 **ARRANGE** the beef slices and asparagus on 4 plates and serve with
the daikon vinegar sauce.

PAN-FRIED GYOZA

YAKI GYOZA

SERVES 4   PREPARATION TIME: 45 MINUTES   COOKING TIME: 20 MINUTES

These little dumplings, known as gyoza, *are very popular in Japan as well as in their country of origin, China. Other minced meat, such as chicken or beef, can also be used, and ready-made gyoza wrappers are available from oriental shops.*

4 large **Chinese leaves**, par-boiled, patted dry and finely chopped

1 tbsp **cornflour**

250g/9oz **minced pork**

2 **spring onions**, finely chopped

1 **garlic** clove, finely chopped

2.5cm/1in piece **root ginger**, peeled and finely chopped

1 tsp **sesame oil**

½ tsp **sea salt** and a pinch freshly ground **black pepper**

24 **gyoza wrappers** (7.5cm/3in in diameter)

plain flour, for dusting

2–3 tbsp **vegetable oil**

lettuce leaves, such as **lollo rosso**

6 tbsp **shoyu** mixed with 4 tbsp **rice vinegar** and 1–2 tsp **chilli oil**, for dipping

1 **WRAP** the chopped Chinese leaves in a clean tea towel and squeeze out the excess water. Put the Chinese leaves, cornflour, pork, spring onions, garlic, ginger and sesame oil in a mixing bowl, season with salt and pepper and mix well.

2 **LAY** 1 gyoza wrapper on a board and spoon about 1 tbsp of the mixture onto it. Wet the edge of the wrapper with water. Fold the gyoza into a half moon shape, sealing the edge with 7–8 gathers. Place on a lightly floured plate with the sealed side up. Repeat with the remaining meat mixture and wrappers.

3 **HEAT** the vegetable oil in a large frying pan over a medium heat and fry half the gyoza, stuffed side down, for 2–3 minutes until the base is golden.

4 **POUR** hot water into the pan until it comes halfway up the sides of the gyoza, cover with a lid and steam-cook over a high heat for 5–6 minutes until nearly all the water has evaporated.

5 **REDUCE** the heat and cook the gyoza, uncovered, for 1 minute to crisp up. Remove, then repeat with the remaining gyoza. Arrange 6 gyoza on each plate with some lettuce. Serve with shoyu mixed with rice vinegar, and a little chilli oil.

GRILLED SKEWERED CHICKEN *YAKITORI*

MAKES **12** SKEWERS   PREPARATION TIME: **25** MINUTES
COOKING TIME: **15** MINUTES

This is the Japanese answer to Malaysian satay, and it is eaten with a sauce that is probably the simplest and least spicy of all satays found in South-east Asia.

6 skinless, boneless **chicken thighs**, quartered

12 small **okra**, trimmed

4 **spring onions**, white part only, each cut into 2 x 4cm/1½in pieces

powdered **sansho** and/or **seven-spice chilli powder**, for sprinkling and dipping (optional)

lemon wedges (optional)

TARÉ SAUCE:

3 tbsp **saké**

4 tbsp **shoyu**

1 tbsp **mirin**

⅔ tbsp **sugar**

1 **SOAK** 12 bamboo skewers in water until ready to use. To make the taré sauce, put the saké, shoyu, mirin and sugar in a small saucepan and bring to the boil. Reduce the heat and simmer, stirring, for about 10 minutes until the sauce has reduced by a third and thickened slightly. Remove from the heat and set aside.

2 **PREHEAT** the grill to medium. Thread 3 chicken pieces tightly together onto 8 of the skewers. Cover the exposed area of the skewers with aluminium foil to prevent them burning. Cook under the grill for 3–4 minutes, then turn and grill for another 2–3 minutes until golden. Reduce the grill to its lowest setting.

3 **REMOVE** the chicken skewers from the grill, baste with the taré sauce and return them to the grill until the sauce has dried. Repeat this process 2–3 times until the chicken is golden brown.

4 **THREAD** 3 pieces of okra and 2 of spring onion, alternately, onto the remaining 4 skewers, protecting the exposed parts with foil, as before. Grill under a low heat for 1–2 minutes each side.

5 **ARRANGE** 1 vegetable and 2 chicken skewers decoratively on each of 4 plates and sprinkle with sansho and/or seven-spice chilli powder, if using. Serve hot, with extra sansho and/or seven-spice chilli powder and lemon wedges, if using.

CHICKEN BALLS WITH EDAMAME
TORI SHINJO TO EDAMAME

SERVES 4   PREPARATION TIME: 15 MINUTES   COOKING TIME: 30 MINUTES

Small, simple dishes feature prominently in Japanese cuisine, and each one can be served separately one after the other or a few items can appear together on one plate. This recipe is a typical example of the latter.

250g/9oz finely **minced chicken**

1 small **egg**, beaten

2 tsp **sugar**

1½ tsp **shoyu**

2 tbsp **vegetable oil**

powdered **sansho**, for sprinkling

100g/3½oz **edamame** pods, cooked in salted water until just tender

coarse **sea salt**

TARÉ SAUCE:
6 tbsp **mirin**

4 tbsp **shoyu**

3 tbsp **saké**

1 **MIX** the chicken, egg, sugar and shoyu together. Using wet hands, divide the mixture into 16 portions of equal size, then roll them into 16 neat balls. Bring a saucepan of water to the boil and cook 4–5 balls at a time, over a medium heat, for 2 minutes until firm; remove using a slotted spoon.

2 **MAKE** the taré sauce by putting the mirin, shoyu and saké in a small saucepan. Bring to the boil, then reduce the heat and leave to simmer for 7–8 minutes until reduced by a third. Remove from the heat and set aside.

3 **HEAT** the oil in a non-stick frying pan over a medium heat. Add the chicken balls and fry for 5–6 minutes, turning occasionally, until light golden, then remove from the pan and turn off the heat.

4 **DIP** the balls, one at a time, into the taré sauce and return them to the hot pan for 3–4 minutes until the sauce has dried on them. Repeat 2–3 times, until the balls are golden brown. Leave to cool, then thread 2 balls at a time on to 8 bamboo skewers. Sprinkle with a little sansho.

5 **ARRANGE** 2 skewers and a quarter of the edamame pods on each plate. Sprinkle the edamame with salt and serve.

DEEP-FRIED CHICKEN WITH SPRING ONION SAUCE *TORI NO KARA-AGE NEGI SOSU-AE*

SERVES 4   PREPARATION TIME: 15 MINUTES, PLUS 45 MINUTES MARINATING
COOKING TIME: 25 MINUTES

Deep-frying was introduced from China, hence this dish's name, kara-age *(meaning "Chinese fry"). This is now established as a popular Japanese home-cooked dish.*

1 tbsp **saké**

1 tbsp **shoyu**

2.5cm/1in piece **root ginger**, grated and juice squeezed out

300g/10½oz skinless, boneless **chicken thighs**, cut into 4cm/1½in cubes

1 **egg**, beaten

cornflour, for dusting

vegetable oil, for deep-frying

red pepper, finely shredded

tarragon sprigs (optional)

SPRING ONION SAUCE:

2 **spring onions**, finely chopped

2 tbsp **sugar**

2 tsp **sesame oil**

2 tbsp each **saké** and **shoyu**

1 **MIX** the saké and shoyu with the ginger juice in a mixing bowl and add the chicken. Rub the sauce into the chicken with your fingers, then leave to marinate for 15 minutes. Stir in the egg and leave for another 15 minutes.

2 **TOSS** the flavoured chicken in the cornflour, shaking off any excess. Heat the oil in a deep-fryer or wok to 170°C/340°F. Deep-fry the chicken cubes, a handful at a time, for 5–6 minutes, turning occasionally, until golden. Lower the heat and deep-fry for a further 3–4 minutes until well cooked. Remove from the oil using a slotted spoon, drain on a wire rack and leave to cool slightly. Reheat the oil to 170°C/340°F, then cook the remaining batches in the same way.

3 **HEAT** the oil to 180°C/350°F and fry the chicken for 1 more minute until the exterior is really crisp. Remove from the oil using a slotted spoon and drain on a wire rack.

4 **MAKE** the spring onion sauce by putting the spring onions, sugar, sesame oil, saké and shoyu in a bowl and mixing well. Arrange the fried chicken on a serving plate and spoon the spring onion sauce over it. Add red pepper and sprigs of tarragon, if using.

ASPARAGUS CHICKEN ROLLS

ASUPARAGASU NO SASAMI-MAKI

SERVES 4   PREPARATION TIME: 35 MINUTES   COOKING TIME: 15 MINUTES

Poultry has played an important part in Japanese cuisine for much longer than red meat. It is also a very versatile ingredient, and rolling and stuffing it makes both the cooking fun to do and the end result beautiful to look at.

4 **chicken breast** fillets, about 650g/1lb 7oz total weight

5 tbsp **saké**

16 **shiso** or **basil** leaves

6 **asparagus** spears, trimmed, halved and par-boiled in lightly salted water

2 tbsp **vegetable oil**

250ml/9fl oz/1 cup **Dashi** (*see page 27*)

1 tbsp **sugar**

1 tbsp **mirin**

4 tbsp **shoyu**

2 tsp **Japanese** or **English mustard**

sea salt and freshly ground **black pepper**

iceberg lettuce leaves, shredded

1 SLICE each chicken fillet in half horizontally, leaving the longest side still attached so the fillet opens up to make a thin, flat sheet, about 10 x 13cm/4 x 5in. Season and sprinkle over 2 tbsp of the saké.

2 SPREAD 4 shiso or several basil leaves on each of the 4 chicken sheets and put 3 asparagus halves on the leaves, parallel with the shortest side. Roll the chicken up tightly and secure with a cocktail stick.

3 HEAT the oil in a frying pan and fry the chicken rolls over a medium heat for 3–4 minutes, turning occasionally, until light golden. Drain on kitchen paper.

4 WARM the dashi, sugar, mirin, ¼ tsp salt and the remaining saké in a clean frying pan, stirring until the sugar dissolves, then add the chicken rolls. Bring back to the boil and simmer gently over a medium heat for 5 minutes until the chicken is cooked. Drain the chicken, reserving the cooking liquid. Cut each chicken roll into 5 rounds diagonally.

5 STRAIN the cooking liquid into a saucepan and heat, then add the shoyu and mustard, stirring until the mustard dissolves.

6 ARRANGE a bed of iceberg lettuce on each plate, put the chicken rolls on top and serve with the mustard sauce.

SEAFOOD IN JELLY *GYOKAI NO ZERI-YOSE*

**SERVES 4   PREPARATION TIME: 25 MINUTES, PLUS UP TO 8 HOURS SETTING
COOKING TIME: 25 MINUTES**

*Prawns, scallops, okra and gingko nuts are attractively set in a savoury jelly to
create a beautiful party dish, which should be made a day before serving.*

6 raw **king prawns** with shells, deveined
  (*see page 19*)

7 tbsp **saké**

1 tsp **sea salt**

8 **scallops**, shelled

350ml/12fl oz/scant 1½ cups **chicken stock**

½ tsp powdered **kanten**

4 tsp light **shoyu**

4½ tsp powdered **gelatine** soaked in
  3 tbsp water

100ml/3½fl oz/scant ½ cup **Dashi** (*see page 27*)

1 tbsp **mirin**

1 tbsp **rice vinegar**

8 **okra**, trimmed, boiled and chopped into
  1cm/½in pieces

12 canned **gingko nuts**, rinsed (optional)

wasabi paste, to serve

a strip **cucumber** skin (optional)

1 **PUT** the prawns in a saucepan and sprinkle over 5 tbsp of the saké and
½ tsp of the salt. Cover with a lid and steam-cook over a medium heat
for 2 minutes. Add the scallops and continue to steam-cook, covered,
for a further 2–3 minutes. Remove from the heat. Peel the prawns and
slice into 1cm/½in long pieces. Cut each scallop into 3–4 pieces.

2 **MAKE** the jelly by heating the chicken stock over a medium heat and
sprinkling in the kanten. Lower the heat and simmer gently, stirring,
for 3 minutes until the kanten dissolves. Season with the remaining
saké and 1 tsp of the shoyu, then remove from the heat and add the
soaked gelatine. Stir well until the gelatine dissolves, then leave to cool.

3 **HEAT** the dashi in a saucepan over a medium heat until lukewarm,
then season with the mirin, remaining shoyu and salt, and the rice
vinegar. Remove from the heat and set aside.

4 **ARRANGE** a quarter of the prawns, scallops, okra and gingko nuts,
if using, in 4 small soup bowls and pour the jelly over them. Refrigerate
for at least 4 hours or overnight until firmly set. Turn out the seafood
jellies onto 4 plates by dipping each bowl into a sink of hot water, placing
a serving plate on top of each bowl, then inverting both plate and bowl,
giving a firm shake. Spoon the dashi sauce over and serve with wasabi
paste enclosed in a strip of cucumber skin, if using.

TARÉ-GRILLED SCALLOPS WITH VINEGARY SALAD *HOTATE NO TARE-YAKI TO SUNOMONO*

SERVES 4   PREPARATION TIME: 20 MINUTES   COOKING TIME: 15 MINUTES

Sweetened with sugar or mirin, the classic taré sauce gives seafood and meat a wonderful golden glow and enriches their flavour when grilled.

12 large **scallops**, shelled

3 tbsp **saké**

a pinch **sea salt**

powdered **sansho**, for sprinkling

pomegranate seeds (optional)

TARÉ SAUCE:

3 tbsp **shoyu**

3 tbsp **mirin**

VINEGARY SALAD:

⅓ **cucumber**, cut into thin half-moons and sprinkled with salt

2 heaped tbsp dried cut **wakame**, soaked in boiling water for 5 minutes

2 tbsp **rice vinegar**

½ tbsp each **sugar**, **shoyu** and **mirin**

1cm/½in piece **root ginger**, peeled and finely shredded

1 **PUT** the scallops in a saucepan and sprinkle with the saké and salt. Cover with a lid and steam-cook over a gentle heat for 3–4 minutes. Remove the pan from the heat and leave the scallops to cool, then make shallow criss-cross cuts on both sides of each scallop.

2 **MAKE** the taré sauce by mixing the shoyu and mirin in a small saucepan. Bring to the boil, then reduce the heat and simmer for 5–6 minutes until the sauce is reduced by half and thickened.

3 **PREHEAT** the grill to low, then cook the scallops for 1 minute on each side. Brush the taré sauce on both sides of the scallops and return to the grill for 1 minute until dry. Repeat this basting and drying once more. Remove the scallops from the heat and keep warm.

4 **SQUEEZE** out the excess water from the cucumber and then from the wakame, then mix them together. Put the rice vinegar, sugar, shoyu and mirin in a bowl and stir well. Pour this sauce over the cucumber and wakame and toss gently.

5 **ARRANGE** 3 scallops on each plate, sprinkle with the sansho and add the pomegranate seeds, if using. Sprinkle the ginger over the cucumber salad and serve with the scallops.

DEEP-FRIED MACKEREL AND STEAMED KABOCHA SQUASH

SABA NO TATSUTA-AGE TO MUSHI KABOCHA

**SERVES 4   PREPARATION TIME: 20 MINUTES, PLUS 30 MINUTES MARINATING
COOKING TIME: 35 MINUTES**

Mackerel is the gem of all fish: it's delicious, relatively cheap and universally available all year round. This fried, ginger- and shoyu-flavoured method of cooking is called tatsuta-age. *You can also use chicken in place of mackerel.*

---

2 **mackerel** fillets. about 300g/10½oz total weight, cut crossways into 1cm/½in thick pieces

¼ small **kabocha squash**, deseeded and cut into 2.5cm/1in square or triangular pieces

plain flour, for dusting

vegetable oil, for deep-frying

coarse **sea salt**

lemon wedges

mint sprigs (optional)

GINGER MARINADE:

2 tbsp **shoyu**

2 tbsp **mirin**

2.5cm/1in piece **root ginger**, peeled and finely grated

1 **MAKE** the ginger marinade by mixing the shoyu, mirin and ginger in a small bowl. Spoon it over the mackerel and leave to marinate for about 30 minutes.

2 **STEAM** the kabocha over a medium heat for 12 minutes until tender, but do not over-cook. Remove from the heat and leave, still covered, for a further 5 minutes. Take the lid off and leave to cool.

3 **DUST** the mackerel slices with flour, one by one, until coated, then shake off any excess.

4 **HEAT** the oil in a deep-fryer or wok to 170°C/340°F. Slide the floured mackerel slices into the hot oil, a few pieces at a time, and deep-fry for 2–3 minutes until golden, turning once or twice. Remove the mackerel from the oil using a slotted spoon and drain on a wire rack.

5 **DIVIDE** the mackerel and the kabocha between 4 plates. Season the kabocha with salt and add lemon wedges and mint sprigs, if using.

DEEP-FRIED SARDINES MARINATED IN SPICY SAUCE *IWASHI NO NANBAN-ZUKE*

SERVES 4   PREPARATION TIME: 15 MINUTES, PLUS 30 MINUTES MARINATING COOKING TIME: 15 MINUTES

Nanban means "southern barbarians", a term used for foreigners in 17th-century Japan. Later, any foreign-, particularly European-, influenced things were called nanban, like this dish due to its deep-frying and use of chilli.

8 **sardines**, about 450g/1lb total weight, gutted

plain flour, for dusting

vegetable oil, for deep-frying

1 **onion**, sliced into rings

½ **red pepper**, deseeded and sliced crossways

¼ **yellow pepper**, deseeded and sliced crossways

1–2 **celery** sticks, sliced diagonally into strips

1 **dried red chilli**, soaked in warm water, deseeded and cut into rings

watercress sprigs

NANBAN SAUCE:

150ml/5fl oz/scant ⅔ cup **rice vinegar**

150ml/5fl oz/scant ⅔ cup **shoyu**

70ml/2¼fl oz/scant ⅓ cup **Dashi** (*see page 27*)

2 tbsp each **sugar** and **saké**

1 MAKE the nanban sauce by putting the vinegar, shoyu, dashi, sugar and saké in a saucepan. Bring to the boil over a medium heat. Remove from the heat and pour into a large bowl or deep, flat dish.

2 DUST the sardines in the flour, one by one, until coated, then shake off any excess.

3 HEAT the oil in a deep-fryer or wok to 170°C/340°F. Slide the floured sardines into the hot oil and deep-fry in batches for 4–5 minutes until cooked and crisp. Remove from the oil using a slotted spoon and immediately put into the hot nanban sauce.

4 ADD the onion, peppers, celery and chilli to the sauce, spoon the sauce over the sardines so that they are covered and leave to marinate for at least 30 minutes.

5 REMOVE the sardines from the nanban sauce. Place 2 sardines on each plate and spoon over the nanban sauce with the vegetables. Add sprigs of watercress and serve.

GOLDEN PRAWNS *EBI NO KIMI-SOBORO AGE*

SERVES **4**   PREPARATION TIME: **20** MINUTES, PLUS **1** HOUR DRYING
COOKING TIME: **20** MINUTES

Prawns are coated in fine granules of hard-boiled egg yolk to give them a gorgeous golden colour. It's a slightly laborious job but not difficult, and is worth the effort for special occasions. The egg granules can be made a few days in advance. You will find this unusual combination of raspberry sauce and prawns a surprisingly good match.

4 hard-boiled **egg yolks**

vegetable oil, for deep-frying

20 raw **king prawns**, par-boiled in their shells for 3–4 minutes, then shelled, leaving the tail intact

cornflour, for dusting

1 **egg white**, beaten and sieved until smooth

RASPBERRY SAUCE:

10 **raspberries**

2 tbsp **saké**

1 tbsp **mirin**

1 tsp **sugar**

1 **PREHEAT** the oven to its lowest setting. Grate the egg yolks using a fine cheese grater onto a sheet of foil laid on a large baking tray. Spread the yolk granules into a thin layer. Put the tray on the lowest rack in the oven and dry the egg slowly for 1 hour. Remove from the oven and leave to dry until ready to use.

2 **HEAT** the oil in a deep-fryer or wok to about 160°C/325°F. Holding the prawns by the tail, dredge each one, body only, with cornflour, then pat off any excess and dip them in the egg white. Dredge the prawns with the egg-yolk granules and gently press so they are evenly covered. Slide the prawns into the oil, in batches, and deep-fry for 1 minute – do not let them brown. Remove using a slotted spoon and drain on a wire rack.

3 **MAKE** the raspberry sauce by puting the raspberries, saké, mirin and sugar in a small saucepan and warming over a medium heat, crushing the raspberries with the back of a spoon to make a smooth sauce. Gently simmer for 3 minutes until the sauce has reduced by a third, then press through a fine-mesh sieve and discard the seeds.

4 **ARRANGE** 5 golden prawns on each plate, spoon the raspberry sauce in a swirl around them and serve.

PRAWN EGG ROLLS WITH RADISH FLOWERS *EBI NO TAMAGO-MAKI TO KABU NO HANA*

SERVES 4   PREPARATION TIME: 35 MINUTES   COOKING TIME: 15 MINUTES

Thin egg sheet is not only useful for wrapping food but also lends a vivid colour to a dish. You will probably need to practise a few times before getting it right, but any failed sheet can be cut into shreds and used as a garnish or in a salad.

300g/10½oz peeled raw large **king prawns**, finely chopped

2 **spring onions**, finely chopped

½ tsp **sea salt**

2 tsp **saké**

1 **egg white**, beaten

2 **Thin Egg Sheets** (*see page 31*)

cornflour, mixed with a little water to make a paste

12 **pickled radish flowers** (*see page 20*)

mitsuba or **watercress** sprigs

1 **POUND** the prawns using a Japanese grinder and pestle (see page 23) or in a food processor until they form a smooth paste. Put the paste in a bowl with the spring onions, salt, saké and egg white and mix well using a fork.

2 **TRIM** about 1cm/½in from both sides of the egg sheets to make 2 square sheets and lay them on a clean moist muslin or tea towel. Spread half the prawn mixture evenly over 1 sheet, leaving a 2.5cm/1in margin at the far side. Pick up the cloth, the nearest side to you, and roll as tightly as possible to the other side. Seal the egg roll with the cornflour paste and wrap tightly in the cloth. Repeat this process using the remaining egg sheet and prawn mixture.

3 **PUT** the wrapped egg rolls on a plate and steam over a medium heat for 15 minutes. Remove the egg rolls from the heat, unwrap them and cut into 1cm/½in thick rounds.

4 **DRAIN** the radish flowers and pat dry with kitchen paper. Finely chop a tiny amount of the cut-off egg sheet and put in the centre as "pollen". Arrange a quarter of the egg roll slices on each plate and serve with the radish flowers and mitsuba or watercress.

TOFU AND PRAWN BALLS *HIRYOZU*

SERVES 4 PREPARATION TIME: 30 MINUTES, PLUS 30 MINUTES DRAINING
COOKING TIME: 25 MINUTES

This dish has its origins in Portugal, hence the unusual name of hiryozu, *which comes from a Portuguese word for a type of deep-fried cake. It's also called* ganmodoki, *meaning "goose look-a-like", due to its texture and appearance.*

1 block **firm tofu**, about 300g/10oz

100g/3oz raw peeled **prawns**, finely chopped

15g/½oz dried **wood ear fungus**, soaked
   in warm water for 15 minutes, then drained,
   trimmed and finely shredded

½ small **carrot**, peeled and cut into 2.5cm/1in strips

1½ tbsp **cornflour**, mixed with 1 tbsp water to
   make a paste

½ **egg**, beaten

sea salt

1 tsp light **shoyu**, plus extra to serve

2 tsp **mirin**

1½ tbsp **sesame seeds**

vegetable oil, for deep-frying

12 canned **gingko nuts**, rinsed

basil leaves

5cm/2in piece **daikon**, peeled and grated, to serve

1 PLACE the tofu block on a cutting board over the sink or on the draining board and put another board, or a flat plate with a weight, on top. Leave for 30 minutes to squeeze out the excess water.

2 POUND the peeled prawns using a Japanese grinder and pestle (see page 23) or in a food processor until they form a smooth paste. Add the drained tofu and pound together.

3 COOK the wood ear fungus and carrot together in boiling water over a medium heat for 1–2 minutes, then drain.

4 MIX the cornflour paste and egg into the tofu mixture, then season with salt, shoyu and mirin. Add the wood ear fungus, carrot and sesame seeds and turn the mixture with a wooden spatula.

5 DIVIDE the mixture into 12 equal pieces. Oil your palm, take 1 portion of tofu and shape into a neat ball the size of a golf ball. Repeat to make 12 balls in total. Push a gingko nut into the centre of each ball.

6 HEAT the oil in a deep-fryer or wok to about 150°C/300°F. Deep-fry the tofu and prawn balls, a few at a time, for 4–5 minutes until golden brown. Remove using a slotted spoon and drain on a wire rack.

7 ARRANGE a bed of basil leaves in each of 4 bowls and place 3 balls on top of each. Serve with the daikon and extra shoyu alongside.

PRAWN AND EGG TERRINE

TAMAGO SHINJO TO HASU NO AMASU-ZUKE

SERVES 4 PREPARATION TIME: 35 MINUTES, PLUS OVERNIGHT MARINATING
COOKING TIME: 45 MINUTES

The three items – one from the sea, one from the field and one from the mountain – arranged on one dish is a traditional kaiseki (Japanese multi-course haute cuisine) way of serving food.

9 raw **king prawns** with shells, deveined
  (*see page 19*)

225g/8oz raw peeled **prawns**, finely chopped

1 **egg** and 3 **egg yolks**

½ tbsp **mirin**

sea salt

2 tbsp cooked red **kidney beans**

red **shiso** sprigs (optional)

lotus root flowers (*see page 20*), to serve
  (optional)

80g/3oz **mangetout**, trimmed and cooked in
  salted boiling water for 1 minute, then drained
  and patted dry, to serve

1 COOK the king prawns in lightly salted boiling water over a medium heat for 4 minutes, then drain and peel the prawns. Set aside.

2 POUND the peeled prawns using a Japanese grinder and pestle (see page 23) or in a food processor until they form a smooth paste. Beat together the egg and 1 of the egg yolks and add to the paste with the mirin and salt, to taste, then continue to grind. Add the kidney beans and mix well so that the beans are spread evenly throughout the mixture.

3 TRANSFER the prawn mixture to a heat-proof container, about 12cm long x 7.5cm wide x 5cm deep/4½ x 3 x 2in, and steam over a medium heat for about 25 minutes until set. Remove from the heat. Beat the 2 remaining egg yolks and pour over the terrine, then arrange the cooked king prawns on top. Return the terrine to the steamer for another 7 minutes, then leave to cool.

4 TURN the prawn and egg terrine out of the container and carefully cut into 4 slices. Add sprigs of red shiso, if desired, then serve with the lotus root flowers, if using, and the mangetout.

THREE DIPS WITH FRESH VEGETABLES

NAMA YASAI NO DIPPU SANSHU

SERVES 4   PREPARATION TIME: 40 MINUTES   COOKING TIME: 15 MINUTES

These three dips look stunning served on a plate with a selection of colourful fresh vegetable sticks, such as cucumber, celery and carrot, and button mushrooms.

185ml/6fl oz/¾ cup **soya milk**

sea salt

a selection of fresh **vegetables**, for dipping

KABOCHA AND MISO DIP:

¼ small **kabocha squash**

1½ tbsp **miso**

TOFU AND SESAME DIP:

3 tbsp **white sesame seeds**, lightly toasted

150g/5½oz **firm tofu**, roughly chopped

1 tsp **sugar**

1 tsp **black sesame seeds**

few drops **chilli oil** (optional)

AVOCADO AND WASABI DIP:

1 small **avocado**, pitted and chopped

1 tbsp **lemon** juice

1–2 tsp **wasabi** paste

1 MAKE the kabocha and miso dip by steaming the kabocha over a medium heat for 15 minutes, then remove from the heat and leave to cool. Scrape the flesh out with a spoon, discarding the skin, and pound it in a Japanese grinder and pestle (see page 23) or in a food processor until it forms a smooth paste. Mix in the miso and 5 tbsp of the soya milk. Transfer to a serving bowl.

2 PREPARE the tofu and sesame dip by grinding the white sesame seeds in a Japanese grinder and pestle or in an electric grinder. Add the tofu and pound together. Stir in 3 tbsp of the soya milk and the sugar, then season with salt to taste. Stir in the black sesame seeds, setting aside a few to garnish, and a few drops of chilli oil, if using. Transfer to a serving bowl and sprinkle with the remaining black sesame seeds.

3 MAKE the avocado and wasabi dip by putting the avocado in a Japanese grinder and pestle or in a food processor and grinding it to a smooth paste. Mix in the lemon juice, remaining soya milk and wasabi and salt to taste. Transfer to a serving bowl.

4 PREPARE a selection of vegetable sticks and button mushrooms, arrange them on a serving plate and serve with the dips.

DEEP-FRIED TOFU WITH DASHI SAUCE *AGEDASHI DOFU*

SERVES 4   PREPARATION TIME: 20 MINUTES, PLUS 30 MINUTES DRAINING
COOKING TIME: 15 MINUTES

This simple but delicious tofu dish is one of the most popular items at Japanese restaurants around the world. For vegetarians, use vegetable stock instead of dashi.

2 blocks **firm tofu**, about 600g/1lb 5oz total weight

3 tbsp **plain flour**

3 tbsp **cornflour**

vegetable oil, for deep-frying

5cm/2in piece **daikon**, peeled and finely grated

2.5cm/1in piece **root ginger**, peeled and finely grated

1 **spring onion**, finely chopped

4 **dill** sprigs (optional)

DASHI SAUCE:

6 tbsp **Dashi** (*see page 27*)

3 tbsp **shoyu**

2 tsp **sugar**

1 PLACE the tofu blocks side by side on a cutting board over the sink or on a draining board and put another board, or a flat plate with a weight, on top. Leave for 30 minutes to squeeze out the excess water.

2 REMOVE the top cutting board or plate and cut each tofu block into 4 large cubes. Mix together the flour and cornflour on a plate, then dredge the tofu in the mixture and shake off any excess.

3 HEAT the oil in a deep-fryer or wok to 180°C/350°F. Gently slide 2 of the tofu pieces into the hot oil and deep-fry over a medium heat for 3–4 minutes, turning a few times, until light golden. Remove the tofu using a slotted spoon and drain on a wire rack. Repeat with the remaining tofu pieces.

4 MAKE the dashi sauce by putting the dashi, shoyu and sugar in a saucepan and heating over a medium heat until the sugar dissolves. Remove from the heat and pour into 4 bowls. Put 2 pieces of tofu in each bowl and top with the daikon and ginger. Add spring onion and dill sprigs, if using, and serve hot.

SQUASH MISO SOUP WITH TOFU AND MANGETOUT *TOFU TO KINUSAYA NO KABOCHA MISOSHIRU*

SERVES 4 PREPARATION TIME: 20 MINUTES COOKING TIME: 20 MINUTES

The nutty flavour of squash gives depth to this humble miso soup, and upgrades it to a superb party dish. This soup can also be served as part of a Western dinner.

250g/9oz **squash** (butternut, squash onion or kabocha), deseeded

20g/¾oz **mangetout**, trimmed and sliced diagonally

4 tbsp **khaki miso**

420ml/14½fl oz/1⅓ cups **Dashi** (*see page 27*)

100g/3½oz **soft tofu**, cut into small cubes

sea salt

5cm/2in piece **spring onion**, green part only, thinly sliced

1 STEAM the squash over a medium heat for 15 minutes until very tender. Remove from the heat and leave, still covered, to cool in the steamer.

2 COOK the mangetout in lightly salted boiling water for 1 minute until just tender. Remove from the heat, drain and place under cold running water to cool quickly. Set aside.

3 SPOON out the flesh from the squash into a Japanese grinder and pestle (see page 23) or a food processor, discarding the outer skin, and pound or process to a smooth purée. Transfer the purée to a large mixing bowl, add the miso and mix well.

4 HEAT the dashi in a saucepan until lukewarm and gradually mix into the squash and miso mixture, 2–3 ladlefuls at a time. Return the mixture to the pan and gently bring to boiling point over a medium heat. Add the tofu to the soup and bring back to the boil, then immediately remove the pan from the heat.

5 POUR the soup into 4 bowls and divide the mangetout slices between the bowls. Serve hot, sprinkled with the sliced spring onion.

AVOCADO MISO SOUP WITH TOMATO AND TURNIP *TOMATO TO KABU NO ABOKADO MISOSHIRU*

SERVES 4   PREPARATION TIME: 15 MINUTES   COOKING TIME: 10 MINUTES

The idea of cooking avocado may sound a little avant-garde, but when mixed into a simple miso soup it gives a subtle green colour and a wonderfully silky texture. Serve hot or cold.

2 small **turnips**

400ml/14½fl oz/scant 1⅔ cups **Dashi** (*see page 27*)

1 ripe **avocado**, pitted and roughly chopped

1 tbsp **lemon** juice

4 tbsp **khaki miso**

2 **tomatoes**

finely chopped **chives**

1 **CUT** the turnips in half crossways and then quarter each half lengthways to make 16 chunky, bite-sized pieces. Put the dashi and turnips in a pan and cook over a medium heat for 5 minutes until the turnips are just tender. Lower the heat to the lowest setting and keep the soup warm.

2 **PLACE** the avocado in a Japanese grinder and pestle (see page 23) or in a food processor and pound or process until smooth. Add the lemon juice and miso and mix well. Stir the mixture into the dashi.

3 **PLUNGE** the tomatoes into boiling water for 30 seconds, then immediately place them under cold running water (this makes peeling easier). Remove the skin and seeds, then cut into chunky pieces of a similar size to the turnip. Add to the avocado miso soup.

4 **BRING** the soup back to nearly boiling point, then remove from the heat. Spoon 2–3 ladlefuls of the soup into 4 bowls. Serve sprinkled with the chives.

ASSORTED VEGETABLE SOUP

KENCHIN JIRU

SERVES 4   PREPARATION TIME: 20 MINUTES   COOKING TIME: 12 MINUTES

This is a traditional, hearty and healthy family dish made with tofu, konnyaku, carrot and satoimo, but you could use other vegetables or even meat.

---

2 dried **shiitake mushrooms**, soaked in 250ml/8fl oz/1 cup warm water for 30 minutes

½ block **konnyaku**, about 125g/4oz (optional)

2 **satoimo**, peeled and cut into 2.5cm/1in rounds or half-moons, if large

1 tbsp **sesame oil**

1 tbsp **vegetable oil**

½ **carrot**, peeled and thinly sliced diagonally

½ **parsnip**, peeled and finely shredded into 5cm/2in strips

460ml/16fl oz/scant 2 cups **Dashi** (*see page 27*)

100g/3½oz **firm tofu**, cut into 2.5cm/1in cubes

1 sheet (20g/¾oz) **thin deep-fried tofu**, halved lengthways and cut into thin strips

1 tbsp **shoyu**

1 tsp **sea salt**

1 **spring onion**, green part only, finely chopped

1 DRAIN the shiitake, reserving the liquid, and cut into thin strips. Tear the konnyaku, if using, into bite-sized pieces using a teaspoon.

2 RINSE the starch off the satoimo, then drain and pat dry with kitchen paper.

3 HEAT a large saucepan or wok over a medium heat. Add the sesame and vegetable oils, then stir-fry the carrot, parsnip, shiitake and konnyaku, if using, over a high heat for 1–2 minutes.

4 ADD the shiitake soaking liquid and the dashi to the pan and bring to the boil. Lower the heat and add the satoimo, the firm tofu and the deep-fried tofu. Season with the shoyu and salt, then continue to cook over a medium heat for another 5 minutes or until all the vegetables are just tender.

5 REMOVE from the heat and serve the soup in bowls, sprinkled with chopped spring onion.

STEAMED EGG CUSTARD SOUP

CHAWAN-MUSHI

SERVES 4   PREPARATION TIME: 15 MINUTES   COOKING TIME: 20 MINUTES

Chawan-mushi *(meaning "bowl-steam")* is an egg soup with various ingredients. It looks stunningly beautiful, but is very easy to make, so is good for parties as well as for family meals. When served plain, without the additional ingredients, it's perfect for infants and the elderly.

450ml/16fl oz/scant 2 cups **Dashi** *(see page 27)*

½ tsp **sea salt**

1 tsp **mirin**

2 tsp **shoyu**

1 tsp **saké**

150g/5½oz skinless **chicken breast** fillet, thinly sliced

4 raw **king prawns**, peeled and deveined *(see page 19)*

3 **eggs**, beaten

4 small **shiitake mushrooms**, stems removed

12 canned **gingko nuts**, rinsed

4 green sprigs such as **mitsuba, basil** or **mint**

1 **HEAT** the dashi in a saucepan with the salt, mirin and 1 tsp of the shoyu until warm, then remove from the heat and leave to cool.

2 **SPRINKLE** half of the saké and the remaining shoyu over the chicken, rub it in and set aside. Sprinkle the remaining saké over the prawns.

3 **PRESS** the eggs through a fine-mesh sieve into a large mixing bowl. Add the cooled dashi and mix well.

4 **ARRANGE** a quarter of the chicken, 1 prawn, 1 shiitake and 3 gingko nuts in each deep soup bowl or large teacup or mug, and gently spoon 2–3 ladlefuls of the egg and dashi mixture into each one.

5 **PLACE** the bowls in a steamer, cover the steamer with a clean tea towel and place a lid loosely on top. Fold the edges of the tea towel over the top of the lid to keep them away from the heat. Steam for 2 minutes over a medium heat, then reduce the heat to the lowest setting and steam for another 15 minutes. Check the progress a few times, making sure bubbles do not form on the surface.

6 **REMOVE** the bowls from the heat and add some green sprigs. Serve hot in winter or ice-cold in summer.

CLEAR SOUP WITH CLAMS AND SOMEN NOODLES *HAMAGURI TO SOMEN NO SUMASHI-JIRU*

SERVES **4** PREPARATION TIME: **15** MINUTES, PLUS **20** MINUTES SOAKING
COOKING TIME: **10** MINUTES

Umami (meaning "savoury") is known as the fifth taste, after sweet, sour, salty and bitter, and it became recognized world-wide only in recent years. Kombu is umami, as are clams, so this soup is one of the finest examples of what umami is all about.

5cm/2in piece dried **konbu**

2 tbsp **saké**

4 large or 24 small **clams** in their shells

1 bunch dried **somen noodles**, about 90g/3¼oz

70g/2½oz **shimeji mushrooms**, trimmed

½ tsp **sea salt**

½ block **soft tofu**, about 150g/5½oz, cut into 8 cubes

mitsuba stems or a handful **cress**

1 CLEAN the konbu with a damp cloth or kitchen paper, then put it in a saucepan with 450ml/16fl oz/scant 2 cups water and the saké and leave to soak for about 20 minutes.

2 SCRUB the shells of the clams with a wire brush and wash under cold running water. Discard any open clams that do not close when tapped.

3 COOK the somen in boiling water following the packet instructions; drain and plunge straight into cold water. Change the water a few times to remove any starch, then drain again. Divide the somen between 4 soup bowls.

4 ADD the clams to the pan with the konbu and water and bring to the boil over a high heat. Remove and discard the konbu and lower the heat. Spoon off the foam from the surface and cook for 2–3 minutes until the clams open (discard any that do not). Add the shimeji and season with salt, then add the tofu. When the tofu is warm, remove the pan from the heat.

5 ARRANGE 1 large clam or 6 small clams, 2 cubes of tofu and a few stems of shimeji decoratively in each bowl. Top each one with 2 ladlefuls of soup, then add mitsuba or cress and serve hot.

HAND-MOULDED SUSHI

NIGIRI ZUSHI

SERVES 4   PREPARATION TIME: 30 MINUTES

The most important factor when making nigiri *is to ensure the rice is the correct temperature and texture so that the whole piece can be picked up easily yet the rice loosens when it is in the mouth.*

---

1 **Japanese Thick Omelette** *(see page 31)*

4 cooked and peeled **king prawns**, slit along the back and opened out

1½ tsp **mirin**

150g/5½oz **tuna** or **salmon** fillet, skinned *(see page 19)*

1½ tsp **balsamic vinegar**

½ recipe quantity **Sushi Rice** *(see page 24)*

4 thin **nori** ribbons, about 0.5 x 10cm/¼ x 4in

2½ tsp **wasabi** paste

1–2 tsp black **caviar** (any kind)

1 tsp **mayonnaise**

¼ small **red onion**, finely shredded

shiso leaves (optional)

Vinegar-pickled Ginger *(see page 28)*, **to serve**

shoyu, to serve

1 **CUT** the omelette crossways into 4 rectangular pieces, each measuring about 5 x 7.5 x 0.5cm thick/2 x 3 x ¼in. Brush the prawns with a little mirin.

2 **SLICE** the tuna neatly into 4 thin pieces of a similar size to the omelette and brush with a little balsamic vinegar.

3 **MOULD** 1 level tablespoonful of the sushi rice into a 1 x 4 x 1cm thick/ ½ x 1½ x ½in rectangular block, using wet hands. Repeat to make 12 rectangular rice blocks.

4 **COVER** 4 of the rice blocks with the omelette and tie with a nori ribbon. Put a little wasabi paste on top of the remaining 8 rice blocks. Cover 4 rice blocks with a prawn and garnish with a dot of caviar on top.

5 **COVER** the remaining 4 rice blocks with the tuna. Mix together ½ tsp wasabi with the mayonnaise and spoon on top of the tuna, then add a few shreds of red onion.

6 **ARRANGE** a couple of shiso leaves on each plate, if using, and add one of each nigiri. Serve with pickled ginger and shoyu.

THIN-ROLLED SUSHI

HOSO-MAKI

SERVES 4 PREPARATION TIME: 45 MINUTES

The thin roll is a good starting point in sushi making. In this recipe, fillings are cut into thin matchsticks for decorative purposes.

1½ **nori** sheets, 20 x 18cm/8 x 7in, the whole one halved crossways

½ recipe quantity **Sushi Rice** (*see page 24*)

1 tsp **wasabi** paste

7.5cm/3in piece **cucumber**, deseeded and cut into thin matchsticks

5cm/2in piece **pickled daikon**, cut into thin matchsticks

2 slices **smoked salmon**, cut into thin strips

Vinegar-pickled Ginger (*see page 28*), to serve

shoyu, to serve

1 PLACE a bamboo sushi mat (see page 23) parallel to you on a work surface and top with one half of a nori sheet, placed crossways. With wet hands, spread a third of the sushi rice in an even layer on the nori, leaving a 2.5cm/1in margin at the far side.

2 SPREAD a small amount of wasabi paste in a horizontal line across the centre of the rice. Place the cucumber on top of the wasabi line in a layer about 1cm/½in thick.

3 PICK up the mat from the near side and roll it over, keeping the cucumber in the centre with your fingers. Lift the upper edge of the mat and roll the rice cylinder on to the rest of the nori. Gently press into a nice square shape.

4 TRANSFER the roll from the mat to a flat container, seam-side down.

5 MAKE 1 more roll in the same way, using the pickled daikon, but without any wasabi, then another with smoked salmon and wasabi. Cut each roll into 8 rounds, using a wet knife, and arrange 2 pieces of each roll, cut-side up, on each plate. Serve with pickled ginger and shoyu.

THICK-ROLLED SUSHI

FUTO-MAKI

SERVES 4   PREPARATION TIME: 45 MINUTES

With five fillings in various colours, this is a truly beautiful party sushi, but it will require a bit of practice before you succeed in making a perfect roll.

250g/9oz **spinach**, blanched in lightly salted water, drained and squeezed to remove the excess water

3 tbsp **shoyu**, plus extra to serve

5–6 dried **shiitake mushrooms**, soaked in 250ml/9fl oz/1 cup warm water for 30 minutes

2 tbsp **sugar**

2 tbsp **mirin**

1 **carrot**, peeled and cut into 2.5cm/1in matchsticks

3 **nori** sheets, 20 x 18cm/8 x 7in

1 recipe quantity **Sushi Rice** (*see page 24*)

6 raw **king prawns**, cooked straight (*see page 19*) and peeled

1 **Thick Japanese Omelette** (*see page 31*), cut lengthways into 1cm/½in thick sticks

Vinegar-pickled Ginger (*see page 28*), to serve

1 **SPRINKLE** the spinach with 2 tsp of the shoyu; set aside.

2 **DRAIN** the shiitake, retaining the soaking liquid, and cut them into thin strips. Put the soaking liquid in a small saucepan with 1 tbsp each of the shoyu, sugar and mirin and heat, stirring. Add the carrot and cook for 2 minutes, then remove using a slotted spoon and transfer to a plate. Add the shiitake to the pan with the remaining shoyu, sugar and mirin and cook for 3–4 minutes. Drain and squeeze the excess liquid from the shiitake. Set aside.

3 **PLACE** a bamboo sushi mat (see page 23) parallel to you on a work surface and top with a nori sheet, placed crossways. With wet hands, spread a third of the sushi rice in an even layer on top of the nori, leaving a 2.5cm/1in margin at the far side.

4 **PUT** 2 prawns in a horizontal line across the centre of the rice. Top with a third of the omelette, spinach (formed into a cylinder), carrot and shiitake. Roll in the same way as for Thin-rolled Sushi (see page 79). Repeat the rolling twice more using the remaining ingredients.

5 **CUT** each roll into 8 rounds, using a wet knife, and divide between 4 plates. Serve with pickled ginger and shoyu.

HAND-ROLLED SUSHI

TEMAKI ZUSHI

SERVES 4   PREPARATION TIME: 15 MINUTES

This is the easiest type of sushi to make, as you just need to chop a few ingredients and let diners help themselves: a perfect fun party dish. Choose fillings with a variety of tastes, textures and colours. The quantities here provide six rolls per person, so for a starter (shown here) use just half the quantities of ingredients.

1 recipe quantity **Sushi Rice** (*see page 24*)

4 raw large **king prawns**, heads removed and deveined (*see page 19*)

4 slices **smoked salmon**, cut into thin strips

7.5cm/3in piece **cucumber**, quartered, deseeded and cut diagonally into thin strips

5cm/2in piece **pickled daikon**, cut diagonally into thin strips

a handful **enoki mushrooms**, trimmed

4 **nori** sheets, 20 x 18cm/8 x 7in, quartered

8 Little Gem **lettuce** leaves

wasabi paste, to serve

shoyu, to serve

1 **TRANSFER** the cooked sushi rice to a serving bowl and cover with a clean damp tea towel while preparing the filling ingredients.

2 **THREAD** each prawn onto a skewer. Blanch in lightly salted boiling water for about 2 minutes until the shell is bright red. Drain and place under cold running water. Remove the skewers and carefully peel the prawns, then cut each in half lengthways.

3 **ARRANGE** the prawns, smoked salmon, cucumber, pickled daikon and enoki on a large serving plate and the nori and lettuce leaves on separate plates, and serve with wasabi and shoyu. Diners place a sheet of nori or a lettuce leaf on their plate, then add some rice and any fillings of their choice before rolling their own *temaki* (hand roll). They should then repeat with the remaining nori, lettuce and fillings, as liked.

CALIFORNIAN REVERSE ROLL

KARIFORUNIA URAMAKI

SERVES 4   PREPARATION TIME: 40 MINUTES

Invented in California, rolled sushi using avocado as its main ingredient is now popular all over the world, even in Japan. Use any ingredients of your choice along with the avocado.

---

2 **nori** sheets, 20 x 18cm/8 x 7in, halved crossways

1 recipe quantity **Sushi Rice** (*see page 24*)

6 tbsp **white sesame seeds**, lightly toasted

10 **seafood sticks**, of which 4 are cut in half

1 **avocado**, peeled, pitted and sliced lengthways into 8 pieces

1 bunch **chives**

6 tbsp **black sesame seeds**, lightly toasted

Vinegar-pickled Ginger (*see page 28*), to serve

shoyu, to serve

1 **PLACE** a cling film-covered bamboo sushi mat (see page 23) parallel to you on a work surface and top with a nori sheet. With wet hands, spread a quarter of the sushi rice in an even layer over the nori. Sprinkle 3 tbsp of the white sesame seeds over the rice.

2 **TURN** the rice bed over on the sushi mat so that the rice side is face down. Place 2½ seafood sticks, 2 avocado slices and about 8 chives in a horizontal row across the bottom of the nori. Roll in the same way as for Thin-rolled Sushi (see page 79). Wrap in the cling film and set aside. Repeat to make 3 more rolls using the remaining ingredients, sprinkling the rice for 1 of the rolls with the remaining white sesame seeds and the rice for the other 2 rolls with the black sesame seeds.

3 **REMOVE** the rolls from the cling film and cut each one into 5 rounds, using a sharp, wet knife. Place a mixture of white and black sesame seed rounds on each of 4 plates. Serve with pickled ginger and shoyu.

PRESSED SUSHI WITH SMOKED TROUT

MASU NO OSHI-ZUSHI

SERVES 4   PREPARATION TIME: 20 MINUTES, PLUS 10 MINUTES MARINATING

Layers of rice and sweet-marinated smoked fish look attractive and enable you to make multiple pieces of sushi in one go — indispensable if you have a large number of people to feed. Pressed sushi is also convenient as it can be made a day ahead.

1 recipe quantity **Sushi Rice** (*see page 24*)

finely grated zest of 1 **lemon**

175g/6oz **smoked trout** or **salmon**, thickly sliced

1 **lime** slice, cut into pieces

1 tbsp finely chopped **parsley** mixed with 2 tsp **caper berries** in vinegar, finely chopped

Vinegar-pickled Ginger (*see page 28*), to serve

shoyu, to serve

MARINADE:

2 tbsp **shoyu**

2 tbsp **saké**

1 tsp **mirin**

1 **SPRINKLE** the cooked sushi rice with half the lemon zest and gently fold in.

2 **MAKE** the marinade by putting the shoyu, saké and mirin in a bowl and mixing well. Add the trout and leave for 10 minutes, then drain. Arrange the trout in an even layer in a wet sushi mould (see page 23), or place in a cling film-lined box container, 20 x 10 x 5cm deep/8 x 4 x 2in, making sure the cling film hangs over the edges. Sprinkle the remaining lemon zest over the trout.

3 **PRESS** the rice with wet hands to form an even layer, about 2.5cm/1in thick, on top of the trout.

4 **COVER** the rice with the wet lid of the sushi mould or the cling film with a piece of cardboard cut to fit inside the container. Place a weight (about 450g/1lb) on top and leave for 30 minutes to a few hours. Remove the sushi from the mould and cut into bite-sized pieces using a wet knife.

5 **ADD** pieces of lime to half the sushi and the parsley and caper mixture to the rest. Arrange on 4 plates and serve with pickled ginger and shoyu.

MACKEREL LOG SUSHI

BATTERA

SERVES 4   PREPARATION TIME: 35 MINUTES, PLUS 3 HOURS SALTING AND 20 MINUTES MARINATING

With the stunningly beautiful silver markings of the mackerel, this sushi cannot fail to draw huge admiration from party guests. Start the preparation early to allow time for the mackerel to rest in the salt.

150g/5½oz/heaped ⅔ cup **sea salt**

2 large **mackerel** fillets, about 450g/1lb total weight

6 tbsp **rice vinegar**

1 recipe quantity **Sushi Rice** *(see page 24)*

4 **bamboo leaves**, to serve (optional)

Vinegar-pickled Ginger *(see page 28)*, to serve

wasabi paste, to serve

shoyu, to serve

1 PUT half the salt in a container, place the mackerel on top, then cover with the remaining salt. Cover and leave in the fridge for 3 hours.

2 WASH the salt off the mackerel, then put the fillets in a shallow dish and pour the rice vinegar over; leave to stand for 20 minutes.

3 DRAIN the fish, remove small bones with a pair of tweezers and carefully remove the outer transparent membrane from the skin with your fingers, leaving the shiny silver pattern intact. Place the fillets, skin-side down, on a cutting board and slice a little off the top to make flat pieces. Lay a fillet, skin-side down, on a cling film-covered bamboo sushi mat.

4 MOULD half the rice, with wet hands, into a firm log shape about the length of each fillet and place it on a fillet. Wrap the sushi in the mat, pressing firmly into a neat log shape. Repeat this process once more with the remaining rice and mackerel. Leave wrapped in the cling film in a dry, cool place for up to 36 hours until ready to serve. (Do not refrigerate.)

5 UNWRAP the sushi logs, slice each one into 1cm/½in thick pieces and place on 4 plates lined with bamboo leaves, if using. Serve with the pickled ginger, wasabi and shoyu.

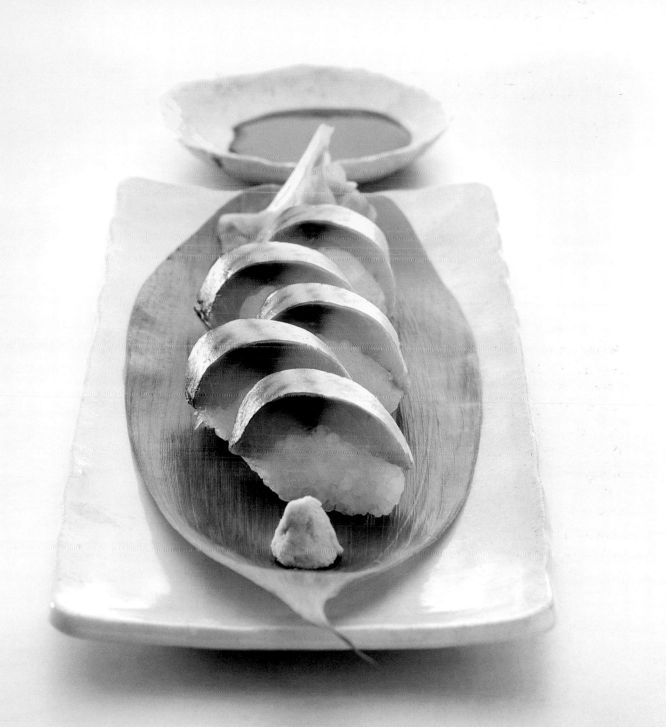

MIXED SUSHI

GOMOKU ZUSHI

SERVES 4 PREPARATION TIME: 15 MINUTES COOKING TIME: 15 MINUTES

This is a very popular and easy-to-make lunchtime party dish that is also good for children's parties and lunchboxes. It normally contains 5 or more items mixed with sushi rice, hence the name, gomoku *(meaning "five kinds").*

2 dried **shiitake mushrooms**, soaked in 150ml/5fl oz/scant ⅔ cup warm water for 30 minutes

2 tbsp **shoyu**

1 tbsp **sugar**

1 tbsp **mirin**

5cm/2in **carrot**, peeled and cut into 2.5cm/1in matchsticks

30g/1oz **mangetout**, trimmed and halved diagonally

sea salt

12 raw peeled **king prawns**

2 tbsp **white sesame seeds**, lightly toasted

1 recipe quantity **Sushi Rice** (*see page 24*)

1 **Thin Egg Sheet** (*see page 31*), cut into 5cm/2in long, very thin strips

2.5cm/1in wide strip of **nori**, finely shredded

1 **DRAIN** the shiitake, reserving the soaking liquid, and cut into thin strips. Put the soaking liquid in a small saucepan with 1 tbsp of the shoyu, the sugar and mirin and heat, stirring until the sugar dissolves. Add the carrot and cook for 2 minutes. Remove using a slotted spoon and transfer to a plate. Add the remaining shoyu and the shiitake to the pan and cook for 3–4 minutes, then drain and set aside.

2 **COOK** the mangetout in lightly salted boiling water for 1 minute until just tender. Remove from the pan using a slotted spoon and place under cold running water, then drain and set aside.

3 **ADD** the prawns to the boiling water in the pan and cook over a high heat for 2 minutes until just cooked, then drain. Place under cold running water, then drain again.

4 **SPRINKLE** the toasted sesame seeds over the sushi rice and gently fold in. Add the carrot, shiitake, mangetout, prawns and half the egg strips to the rice and fold in lightly. Divide the mixed rice between 4 plates, sprinkle with the remaining egg strips and the nori and serve.

FRIED TOFU PARCEL SUSHI

INARI-ZUSHI

MAKES **12** PREPARATION TIME: **25** MINUTES COOKING TIME: **20** MINUTES

It doesn't look like any other sushi, but the traditional use of thin deep-fried tofu to wrap sushi rice is a most interesting and creative idea. It was probably developed for bento (lunchboxes) or for picnics, as the parcel prevents the rice from drying out.

6 **thin deep-fried tofu** sheets

2 tbsp **black** or **white sesame seeds**, lightly toasted

1 recipe quantity **Sushi Rice** *(see page 24)*

shiso leaves (optional)

Vinegar-pickled Ginger *(see page 28)* (optional)

COOKING SAUCE:

150ml/5fl oz/scant ⅔ cup **saké**

90g/3¼oz/scant ½ cup **sugar**

5 tbsp **shoyu**, plus extra to serve

sea salt

1 **PUT** the thin deep-fried tofu sheets in a heatproof bowl and pour over plenty of boiling water to draw out the oil. Drain and squeeze out the excess water when cool enough to handle. Cut each sheet of tofu in half crossways and carefully open up to make 12 pouches.

2 **MAKE** the cooking sauce by putting the saké, sugar, shoyu and salt to taste in a saucepan. Add 150ml/5fl oz/scant ⅔ cup water and bring to the boil, stirring to dissolve the sugar. Add the tofu sheet halves and bring back to the boil, then lower the heat and simmer for about 15 minutes until they are amber in colour. Remove the pan from the heat and leave the tofu to cool in the sauce.

3 **SPRINKLE** the sesame seeds and about 3 tbsp of the cooking sauce over the rice and fold in gently. Divide the rice into 12 equal balls.

4 **DRAIN** the tofu and squeeze out the excess liquid. Stuff a ball of rice into each parcel, then neatly fold in the edge.

5 **MAKE** a bed of shiso leaves, if using, on 4 small plates and place 3 parcels on each one. Add some pickled ginger, if using, and serve with shoyu.

ASSORTED SASHIMI

SASHIMI MORIAWASE

SERVES 4   PREPARATION TIME: 35 MINUTES, PLUS 40 MINUTES
SALTING/MARINATING

It's essential to use extremely fresh fish when making sashimi, so do check with your fishmonger. Here, a typical assortment of fish is used, but you can also try any flatfish, sea bream or shellfish.

1 small **mackerel**, 150–200g/5½–7oz, filleted

sea salt

1 **sea bass**, filleted and skinned (*see page 19*)

150g/5½oz **tuna** steak (ideally blue-fin)

150g/5½oz **salmon** fillet, skinned (*see page 19*)

shiso leaves (optional)

7.5cm/3in piece **daikon**, peeled and thinly shredded (optional)

wasabi paste, to serve

shoyu, to serve

MARINADE:

250ml/9fl oz/1 cup **rice vinegar**

1 tbsp **sugar**

1 tbsp **shoyu**

1 LAY the mackerel fillets in an even layer in a container and cover with plenty of salt, then leave for 30 minutes. Wash off the salt under cold running water and pat the mackerel dry with kitchen paper; set aside.

2 MAKE the marinade by putting the vinegar, sugar and shoyu in a shallow dish and mixing well. Add the mackerel and leave to marinate for 10 minutes.

3 DRAIN the mackerel, remove small bones with a pair of tweezers and carefully remove the outer transparent membrane from the skin with your fingers, leaving the shiny silver pattern intact. Slice 4 neat pieces, about 1cm/½in wide, crossways from each fillet (see page 19).

4 CUT each sea bass fillet crossways into 4 neat pieces, about 1cm/½in thick. Slice the tuna and salmon into 8 pieces, about 6 x 3 x 1cm thick/ 2½ x 1¼ x ½in.

5 MAKE a bed of shiso leaves, if using, on 4 plates and put slices of the mackerel, sea bass, tuna and salmon on top. Add daikon, if using, and serve with wasabi and shoyu.

SEARED BONITO SASHIMI

SHIN KATSUO NO TATAKI

SERVES 4   PREPARATION TIME: 15 MINUTES   COOKING TIME: 5 MINUTES

Katsuo (bonito) caught in May is called "first" katsuo because the fish swim near Japanese shores in late spring on their way north, and are most cherished. Lightly seared outside but pink inside, tataki *is the best way to appreciate the first katsuo.*

---

1 tbsp **vegetable oil**

450g/1lb **bonito** fillet with skin or **tuna** fillet (ideally blue-fin)

7.5cm/3in piece **daikon**, peeled and finely shredded

1 bunch **parsley**, finely chopped

DRESSING:

1 **garlic** clove, finely grated

2.5cm/1in piece **root ginger**, peeled and finely grated

3 tbsp **lime** juice

5 tbsp **shoyu**

1 tsp **sugar**

1 **HEAT** the vegetable oil in a frying pan and sear the bonito, skin-side down, over a high heat for 1–2 minutes. Turn the bonito over and sear the other side for 1 minute until the outside is golden but the centre is still pink. Immediately remove the pan from the heat and plunge the bonito into a bowl of cold water with ice cubes. Drain the bonito and pat dry with kitchen paper, then cut neatly into bite-sized cubes. Put in a large mixing bowl.

2 **MAKE** the dressing by putting the garlic, ginger, lime juice, shoyu and sugar in a bowl and stirring well until the sugar dissolves. Sprinkle half of the dressing over the bonito and toss lightly with your hands. Cover and refrigerate while you prepare the daikon and parsley.

3 **REFRESH** the daikon in cold water, then drain. Sprinkle the parsley over the bonito and mix together lightly.

4 **ARRANGE** the daikon in the centre of 4 plates and top with the bonito. Sprinkle the remaining dressing over the bonito and serve.

MACKEREL SASHIMI WITH
SEA VEGETABLES *SHIME SABA TO KAISO SALADA*

**SERVES 4 PREPARATION TIME: 30 MINUTES, PLUS 30 MINUTES MARINATING
COOKING TIME: 10 MINUTES**

*Simple "curing" in vinegar takes the humble fresh mackerel to a new dimension.
This vinegar dressing, called tosa-zu, is one of the most frequently used of all
Japanese dressings.*

250ml/9fl oz/1 cup **Dashi** (*see page 27*)

5 tbsp **rice vinegar**

200ml/7fl oz/¾ cup plus 2 tbsp **shoyu**

1 tsp **sugar**

a handful **dried bonito flakes**

20 baby **turnips**, halved and soaked in salted water
    for 10 minutes, drained

1 **mackerel**, 350–400g/12–14oz, filleted

3 tbsp **rice vinegar**

1 packet (10g/⅓oz) **dried mixed sea
    vegetable salad**, soaked in water for
    10 minutes

5cm/2in piece **root ginger**, grated and juice
    squeezed out

1 MIX the dashi, rice vinegar, 5 tbsp of the shoyu and sugar in a small
saucepan and bring to the boil. Remove from the heat, add the dried
bonito flakes and leave for 5 minutes, then strain into a bowl. Discard
the dried bonito flakes and leave the vinegar dressing to cool.

2 POUR a third of the dressing into a bowl, then add the turnips to the
remaining dressing in the pan and marinate for at least 30 minutes.

3 REMOVE all the small bones from the mackerel using tweezers and
also remove the outer transparent membrane from the mackerel skin
carefully with your fingers, leaving the shiny silver pattern intact. Cut
the fillets crossways into thin, bite-sized slices (see page 19). Put the
mackerel slices on a flat plate, sprinkle with rice vinegar and set aside.

4 DRAIN the mixed sea vegetable salad and squeeze out the excess water.
Pour the reserved vinegar dressing over and toss lightly.

5 MIX together the remaining shoyu and the ginger juice in a bowl, add
the mackerel and toss. Serve the mackerel on a bed of the sea vegetable
salad with the turnips alongside or in separate dishes.

PRESSED SEA BASS SASHIMI HAKATA-STYLE *SUZUKI NO HAKATA-OSHI*

SERVES 4   PREPARATION TIME: 30 MINUTES, PLUS 10 MINUTES SOAKING COOKING TIME: 5 MINUTES

The taste and texture of the lightly cured sea bass with the cucumber and herbs makes this dish quite unlike anything you might imagine from raw fish. It's also fun to make!

1 large **sea bass**, about 700g/1lb 9oz, filleted, skinned and each fillet sliced in half horizontally to make 4 thin pieces

100ml/3½fl oz/scant ½ cup **rice vinegar**

1 **cucumber**

sea salt

2.5cm/1in piece **root ginger**, peeled and cut into thin strips

shiso leaves or handful **basil** leaves

bamboo leaves (optional)

lime slices

DRESSING:

4 tbsp **rice vinegar**

4 tbsp **Dashi** (*see page 27*)

2 tbsp **shoyu**

1½ tsp **sugar**

1 PAT dry the sea bass using kitchen paper and put it in a dish. Pour the rice vinegar over and leave to marinate for a few minutes.

2 SLICE 4 very thin, long strips from the cucumber using a vegetable peeler, discarding the first strip with the skin. Soak the strips in salted water for 10 minutes until wilted; drain and pat dry with kitchen paper.

3 PUT a large sheet of cling film on a cutting board and lay a piece of sea bass fillet flat in the centre. Place half of the ginger and 2 strips of the cucumber over the fillet and lay a few shiso or basil leaves evenly on top. Cover with a second piece of sea bass and wrap in the cling film. Repeat this process using the remaining 2 pieces of fish, ginger, cucumber and shiso. Put a board on top of the sea bass and press down for a few minutes.

4 MAKE the vinegar dressing by putting the vinegar, dashi, shoyu and sugar in a saucepan and simmering over a medium heat for a few minutes until the sugar dissolves. Remove from the heat and leave to cool.

5 UNWRAP the sea bass and cut into neat slices, about 5 x 2.5cm/2 x 1in. Put a bamboo leaf, if using, on 4 plates and arrange the sea bass on top. Add lime slices and serve with the dressing.

TURBOT SASHIMI SALAD

HIRAME NO SASHIMI SALADA

SERVES 4   PREPARATION TIME: 20 MINUTES   COOKING TIME: 5 MINUTES

This is a sashimi salad for everyone; it's very easy to make – even children can help – and is delicious to eat. Instead of turbot, you can use any other flatfish, such as sea bream, Dover or lemon sole, or shellfish.

1 small **turbot**, about 600g/1lb 5oz, filleted, halved lengthways and skinned (*see page 19*)

2 tbsp **rice vinegar**

sea salt

125g/4oz **basil** leaves

cress, to garnish

1 tbsp **white sesame seeds**, lightly toasted

DRESSING:

juice of 1 **lemon**

1½ tsp **wasabi** paste

2 tbsp **shoyu**

2 tbsp **saké**

1 tsp **sesame oil**

1 **PLUNGE** the turbot fillets, one by one, into boiling water over a high heat and boil for 30 seconds, then plunge into ice-cold water to cool and stop the cooking. Pat dry with kitchen paper.

2 **SLICE** the fillets crossways into 1cm/½in wide sashimi pieces (see page 19), inserting the blade diagonally against the cutting board. Sprinkle the rice vinegar over the turbot and season with salt; set aside

3 **MAKE** the dressing by putting the lemon juice, wasabi, shoyu, saké and oil in a bowl. Stir well to dissolve the wasabi paste and season to taste.

4 **PUT** the basil leaves in a mixing bowl, pour over half the dressing and toss lightly. Divide the basil salad between 4 plates. Arrange the turbot decoratively on top of the basil, then neatly scatter some cress on top. Pour the remaining dressing over the fish, sprinkle with the sesame seeds and serve.

BEEF STEAK WITH SESAME MISO SAUCE *WAFU STEAK GOMA-DARE SOE*

SERVES 4   PREPARATION TIME: 10 MINUTES   COOKING TIME: 25 MINUTES

The sesame miso sauce adds a different dimension to a simple pan-fried steak. Take the meat out of the fridge 30 minutes before cooking for the best result.

---

3 tbsp **vegetable oil**

4 sirloin or rump **beef steaks**, about 200g/7oz each

½ **aubergine**, cut into 1cm/½in thick half-moons

2 **courgettes**, trimmed and cut diagonally into 1cm/½in thick slices

⅛ small **kabocha squash**, deseeded and cut into 1cm/½in thick fan-shaped slices

sea salt and freshly ground **black pepper**

2 tsp **sesame seeds**, lightly toasted

watercress sprigs

SESAME MISO SAUCE:

3 tbsp **tahini** (sesame seed paste)

2 tbsp **khaki miso**

1 tbsp **mirin**

1 tsp **shoyu**

1 tbsp **lemon** juice

4 tbsp **Dashi** *(see page 27)*

1 **HEAT** 1 tbsp of the oil in a large frying pan and spread evenly by tilting the pan. Cut 2 slits into the fat of each steak, then season the steaks with a little salt and pepper. Fry the steaks over a high heat for 2–5 minutes on each side until both sides are browned and cooked to your liking. Set aside and keep warm.

2 **WIPE** the frying pan with kitchen paper and add another 1 tbsp of the oil. Fry the aubergine, courgette and kabocha slices, in batches, adding a little more oil in between, until they are cooked and light golden. Remove from the pan and keep warm.

3 **MAKE** the sesame miso sauce by putting the tahini, miso, mirin, shoyu, lemon juice and dashi in a bowl. Stir well, then divide the sauce between 4 small bowls.

4 **SLICE** each steak diagonally into 2cm/1in wide pieces and place 1 sliced steak on each of 4 plates. Sprinkle the steaks with the sesame seeds and add a sprig of watercress, then serve with the vegetables and some sesame miso sauce. Serve extra sauce in small bowls.

SUKIYAKI

SUKIYAKI

SERVES 4   PREPARATION TIME: 20 MINUTES   COOKING TIME: 10 MINUTES

Sukiyaki *(beef and vegetables cooked in a shallow cast-iron pan at the table) is for everyone, young and old: it's easy, quick and fun to cook, as well as nutritious and delicious to eat.*

450g/1lb very thinly sliced sukiyaki or sirloin **beef**

2 thin **leeks**, cut diagonally into 1cm/½in slices

250g/9oz **spinach**, tough stalks discarded and leaves roughly cut if large

1 bunch **shimeji mushrooms**, trimmed

8 **shiitake mushrooms**, stems trimmed

1 block **firm tofu**, about 300g/10½oz, cut into 2.5cm/1in cubes

200g/7oz **shirataki**, roughly cut (optional)

5cm/2in piece **beef fat** or 1 tbsp **vegetable oil**

4 organic **eggs** (optional)

COOKING SAUCE:

200ml/7fl oz/scant 1 cup **Dashi** (*see page 27*)

6 tbsp **saké**

6 tbsp **mirin**

6 tbsp **shoyu**, plus extra to taste

1 **ARRANGE** the beef on a serving plate, then place the leeks, spinach, shimeji, shiitake, tofu and shirataki on a separate large serving plate.

2 **MAKE** the cooking sauce by putting the dashi, saké, mirin and shoyu in a jug and mixing well.

3 **PLACE** a cast-iron frying pan on a portable gas ring or electric hotplate on the table. Have the plates of raw ingredients and the jug of sauce to hand.

4 **MELT** the beef fat or heat the vegetable oil in the pan. Cook a few slices of the beef first, then add some of the other ingredients and pour in some of the cooking sauce. (When the sauce thickens or evaporates, add some more sauce.) Check the taste and add more shoyu or water, if you like.

5 **BEAT** the eggs, if using, and divide between 4 small bowls. Diners serve themselves by taking pieces of the fried beef and vegetables and either eating them as they are or dipping them into the egg first, if they like. Continue to fry the beef and vegetables in the pan as and when more pieces are needed.

JAPANESE BEEF CURRY

WAFU BEEF CURRY

SERVES 4   PREPARATION TIME: 15 MINUTES   COOKING TIME: 35 MINUTES

Curry was introduced to Japan via England in the middle of the 19th century. Its popularity owes much to the Japanese invention of a curry roux for making a sauce. Curry roux is available at oriental supermakets.

2 tbsp **vegetable oil**, plus extra if necessary

600g/1lb 5oz sirloin **beef**, cut into bite-sized cubes

2 **onions**, thinly sliced

2 **carrots**, peeled and chopped into bite-sized pieces

2 **potatoes**, peeled and chopped into bite-sized pieces

125g/4oz prepared Japanese **curry roux**, cut into small pieces

2 tbsp **shoyu**, to taste (optional)

4 **parsley** sprigs (optional)

cooked **basmati rice**, to serve

1 **HEAT** the oil in a deep saucepan and stir-fry the beef over a high heat for 2 minutes until browned all over. Remove from the pan with a slotted spoon.

2 **REDUCE** the heat to medium, add a little more oil to the pan, if necessary, and stir-fry the onions for about 15 minutes until golden. Add the carrots and potatoes and stir-fry for another 2 minutes.

3 **ADD** 700ml/24fl oz/scant 3 cups water to the pan and bring to the boil. Return the beef to the pan and simmer gently over a low heat for 5–7 minutes until cooked.

4 **REMOVE** the pan from the heat, then stir in the roux until it has dissolved. Return the pan to a medium heat and simmer gently for about 5 minutes, stirring continuously, until the sauce thickens.

5 **ADD** a little shoyu to taste, if you like, and sprigs of parsley, if using, then serve with basmati rice.

SIMMERED BEEF WITH POTATO

NIKU-JAGA

SERVES 4   PREPARATION TIME: 25 MINUTES   COOKING TIME: 35 MINUTES

Despite being a simple, unsophisticated peasant dish, niku-jaga *(an abbreviation of meat and potato) is still alive and kicking in today's affluent society. It's normally cooked with just the two main ingredients, literally, but here green beans are added for their bite as well as their colour.*

85g/3oz **green beans**, cut into about 3cm/1½in pieces

1 tbsp **sesame oil**

1 **onion**, halved and thinly sliced into half-moons

1 tbsp **vegetable oil**

300g/10½oz sirloin **beef**, thinly sliced and cut into 5cm/2in long pieces

4 **potatoes**, peeled, quartered and soaked in water

450ml/16fl oz/scant 2 cups **Dashi** (*see page 27*)

3 tbsp **saké**

3 tbsp **sugar**

1 tbsp **mirin**

5 tbsp **shoyu**

sea salt

2.5cm/1in piece **root ginger**, peeled and finely shredded

1 **BOIL** the green beans in lightly salted boiling water for 2 minutes, then remove from the heat, drain and place under cold running water to cool quickly. Drain and set aside.

2 **HEAT** the sesame oil in a deep saucepan and stir-fry the onion over a high heat for about 3 minutes until softened. Remove the onion from the pan and set aside.

3 **ADD** the vegetable oil to the pan, then stir-fry the beef over a medium heat for 3–4 minutes until it turns pale. Drain the potatoes, add them to the pan and continue to stir-fry for a further minute. Return the onion to the pan.

4 **POUR** the dashi, saké, sugar, mirin and shoyu into the pan, stir, cover with a lid and bring to the boil. Remove any scum from the surface, lower the heat slightly and simmer for about 20 minutes, covered, turning from bottom to top once, or until most of the liquid is absorbed.

5 **ADD** the green beans about 5 minutes before the end of the cooking time. Divide the meat and vegetables between 4 bowls and serve with shredded ginger.

SIMMERED PORK WITH KABOCHA

BUTANIKU TO KABOCHA NO NITSUKE

SERVES 4   PREPARATION TIME: 15 MINUTES   COOKING TIME: 20 MINUTES

With its sweet, nutty flavour and dense texture, kabocha is the best of all squashes, and its rich, orange colour glows in any dish. Unlike other squashes and pumpkins, kabocha's skin is edible and delicious.

3 tbsp **sesame oil**

1 **red pepper**, quartered, deseeded and sliced lengthways

4 **pork loin steaks**, about 800g/1lb 12oz total weight, fat trimmed, cut into bite-sized pieces

½ **kabocha squash**, deseeded and cut into bite-sized pieces

2 tsp **sesame seeds**, lightly toasted, to serve (optional)

COOKING SAUCE:

3 tbsp **sugar**

125ml/4fl oz/½ cup **saké**

5 tbsp **shoyu**

1 **HEAT** 2 tbsp of the sesame oil in a frying pan and stir-fry the red pepper over a medium heat for 1 minute. Remove the pepper from the pan using a slotted spoon and set aside.

2 **ADD** the remaining sesame oil to the pan and stir-fry the pork over a high heat for 2–3 minutes until it turns pale. Add the kabocha and continue to stir-fry for a further minute.

3 **MAKE** the cooking sauce by putting the sugar, saké and shoyu in a small bowl with 150ml/5fl oz/scant ⅔ cup water and stirring until the sugar dissolves. Add to the pan and bring to the boil, then lower the heat and simmer gently, covered with a lid, for 10 minutes. Remove the pan from the heat and leave to stand, still covered, for 2–3 minutes.

4 **STIR** in the red pepper, then divide the pork and vegetables between 4 dishes and serve sprinkled with sesame seeds, if using.

GINGER PORK WITH ROCKET SALAD

BUTANIKU NO SHOGA-YAKI

SERVES 4   PREPARATION TIME: 15 MINUTES, PLUS 10 MINUTES MARINATING
COOKING TIME: 10 MINUTES

Inspired by Chinese cooking, this stir-fried gingered pork is one of the most popular, long-established dishes. It's very quick to make, quite filling and inexpensive – making it an ideal family meal.

4 **pork loin steaks**, each about 250g/9oz, cut crossways into 5 x 2.5cm/2 x 1in wide strips

½ **fennel**, thinly sliced into 5cm/2in long strips

a handful **lollo rosso** leaves

60g/2¼oz **rocket** leaves

1 tbsp **lemon** juice

2 tbsp **vegetable oil**

sea salt and freshly ground **black pepper**

GINGER MARINADE:

5cm/2in piece **root ginger**, grated and juice squeezed out

3 tbsp **shoyu**

2 tbsp **saké**

2 tbsp **mirin**

1 MAKE the ginger marinade by putting the ginger, shoyu, saké and mirin in a shallow dish and mixing well. Add the pork strips and leave to marinate for 10 minutes.

2 PUT the fennel, lollo rosso and rocket in a mixing bowl, sprinkle with lemon juice and season lightly with salt and pepper.

3 HEAT the oil in a frying pan and add the pork and its marinade. Stir-fry over a medium heat for 5–6 minutes until the meat turns pale. Transfer the meat to a plate using a slotted spoon.

4 TURN up the heat and cook any remaining marinade in the pan over a high heat for a further minute, or until thickened to a sauce. Return the pork to the pan and toss quickly so that the pork strips are evenly coated in the sauce.

5 ARRANGE a quarter of the mixed salad in the centre of each of 4 plates and place the pork around the salad. Spoon some of sauce over the pork and serve the rest separately.

DEEP-FRIED PORK STEAK

TONKATSU

SERVES 4   PREPARATION TIME: 20 MINUTES   COOKING TIME: 30 MINUTES

Tonkatsu is one of the national favourites in home cooking. This is an authentic, easy recipe. Tonkatsu sauce, which contains fruits, vegetables, spices and shoyu, is available in bottles at Japanese supermarkets.

4 **pork loin steaks**, each about 200g/7oz

vegetable oil, for deep-frying

dried **breadcrumbs**, for coating

300g/10½oz **white cabbage**, finely shredded

2 **tomatoes**, peeled and cut into wedges

4 **lemon** wedges

sea salt and freshly ground **black pepper**

tonkatsu sauce, to serve

watercress sprigs

BATTER:

1 **egg**, beaten

1 tbsp **plain flour** mixed with 1 tbsp water, plus extra flour for coating

1 FLATTEN the pork gently, using a meat mallet, to tenderize it. Make a few slits in the fat.

2 MAKE the batter by whisking together the egg and flour mixture in a large bowl until smooth.

3 HEAT the vegetable oil in a deep-fryer or wok to 160°C/325°F.

4 SEASON the pork with salt and pepper, dust with flour and shake off any excess. Dip the pork into the egg batter, then the breadcrumbs, gently pressing them into the steaks. Slowly slide the steaks into the hot oil, 2 at a time, and fry for 1–2 minutes, then lower the heat and continue to fry over a medium heat for a further 9–10 minutes until golden all over. Using a slotted spoon, remove the pork steaks and drain on a wire rack. Keep them warm while you cook the remaining 2 steaks.

5 CUT each pork steak crossways into 2.5cm/1in thick slices. Divide the cabbage between 4 plates, then arrange the pork alongside with the tomato and lemon wedges. Spoon the tonkatsu sauce alongside or over the pork and add some watercress.

SIMMERED VEGETABLES WITH CHICKEN

IRI-DORI

SERVES 4   PREPARATION TIME: 20 MINUTES   COOKING TIME: 25–30 MINUTES

Simmered vegetables and chicken make a simple, hearty and nutritious dish for the family.

---

6 tbsp **saké**

4 tbsp **shoyu**

450g/1lb **chicken thigh** meat, cut into small pieces

4 small dried **shiitake mushrooms**, soaked in 250ml/9fl oz/1 cup warm water for 30 minutes

120g/4¼oz **lotus root**, cut into thin half-moons

2 tbsp **rice vinegar**

2 tbsp **vegetable oil**

2 tbsp **mirin**

½ tsp **sea salt**

1 **carrot**, peeled and cut into bite-sized pieces

150g/5oz cooked **bamboo shoots**, drained and cut into bite-sized pieces

3 tbsp **sugar**

½ tsp **dashi** granules

70g/2½oz **mangetout**, trimmed, halved and cooked in salted boiling water for 1 minute

1 RUB 2 tbsp of the saké and 1½ tbsp of the shoyu into the chicken and set aside. Drain the shiitake, reserving the liquid, and trim the stems.

2 SOAK the lotus root in 250ml/9fl oz/1 cup water with the rice vinegar.

3 HEAT 1 tbsp of the oil in a large saucepan and stir-fry the chicken over a medium heat for 2 minutes. Add the remaining saké and shoyu to the pan along with the mirin and salt and stir-fry for a further 5–6 minutes until the chicken is cooked. Transfer to a bowl with any juices.

4 ADD the remaining oil to the pan and stir-fry the carrot, bamboo shoots and shiitake for 2–3 minutes until they begin to turn tender, then stir in the sugar. Add the shiitake soaking liquid and the dashi granules to the pan.

5 PUT a lid on the pan and bring to the boil, then reduce the heat and simmer over a medium heat for 7–8 minutes, stirring occasionally. Drain the lotus root and add it to the pan along with the chicken and cook for a further 10 minutes or until the juices evaporate.

6 STIR in the mangetout, then divide the vegetables and chicken between 4 bowls and serve.

SOUP-STEAMED DUCK

MUSHI GAMO

SERVES 4   PREPARATION TIME: 20 MINUTES
COOKING TIME: 25–30 MINUTES

In this recipe, the duck is seared first to reduce its oiliness, then steamed in a lightly flavoured soup that gently cooks the meat. The result is a remarkably tender, delicately flavoured duck dish.

---

4 **duck breasts**, about 200g/7oz each, excess fat trimmed

1 tbsp **vegetable oil**

1 **carrot**, peeled and thinly sliced

1 **onion**, thinly sliced

1 **celery** stick with leaves, thinly sliced

1–2 tbsp **shoyu**

1 tbsp **mirin**

1 box **cress**, trimmed

STEAMING BROTH:

8 tbsp **shoyu**

4 tbsp **mirin**

670ml/23fl oz/2⅔ cups **Dashi** (*see page 27*)

½ **chicken stock cube**

4 tbsp **saké**

1 SCORE several slits in the duck skin. Heat the oil in a large frying pan and fry the duck breasts, skin-side down, over a high heat for 3–4 minutes until golden. Turn and fry for another 1–2 minutes. Remove the duck from the pan using a slotted spoon and put in a heatproof bowl.

2 MAKE the steaming broth by putting the shoyu, mirin, dashi, stock cube and saké in a saucepan and mixing well. Heat gently, stirring, until the stock cube dissolves. Remove from the heat and pour the broth over the duck breasts.

3 ADD the carrot, onion and celery to the bowl, cover with cling film and put in a steamer. Steam over a high heat for 10 minutes, then leave to cool.

4 POUR 250ml/9fl oz/1 cup of the broth into a small saucepan, add more shoyu to taste and the mirin and bring to the boil. Lower the heat and simmer for 5–10 minutes until the broth has reduced by a third. Remove from the heat and keep warm.

5 DRAIN the duck breasts, discarding the vegetables, and cut them crossways into 2cm/¾in thick slices. Arrange alongside the cress, spoon some of the broth over the duck and serve with extra broth on the side.

MACKEREL SIMMERED IN MISO

SABA NO MISO-NI

SERVES 4   PREPARATION TIME: 15 MINUTES   COOKING TIME: 20 MINUTES

Miso, with its distinctive taste, smell and dense texture, goes well with other ingredients with equally prominent features. Mackerel is one such ingredient. Here's an all-time favourite with Japanese families.

2 **mackerel**, about 600g/1lb 5oz total weight, filleted

2 tbsp **vegetable oil**

2 thin **leeks** or 5 **spring onions**, diagonally sliced

5cm/2in piece **root ginger**, peeled and thinly sliced

5 tbsp **khaki miso**

100g/3½oz **rocket** leaves

COOKING SAUCE:

7 tbsp **saké**

3 tbsp **sugar**

2 tsp **shoyu**

1 SCORE criss-cross cuts on the skin of each mackerel fillet and cut each fillet into 3 slices crossways.

2 HEAT a large frying pan, add the oil and fry the leeks over a medium heat for 1–2 minutes until slightly golden. Remove using a slotted spoon and set aside.

3 MAKE the cooking sauce by mixing the saké, sugar and shoyu with 350ml/12fl oz/scant 1½ cups water. Add it to the frying pan and bring to the boil, stirring until the sugar dissolves. Add the mackerel, skin-side down. The sauce should come halfway up the sides of the mackerel; if it doesn't, add extra water, saké, sugar and shoyu in proportional amounts.

4 SCATTER the ginger slices over the sauce. Return to the boil and spoon the sauce over the fish. Lower the heat and simmer for about 10 minutes.

5 DILUTE the miso with some of the sauce and add it to the pan. Stir gently, then add the leeks. Simmer for a further 4–5 minutes until the sauce thickens.

6 PUT some rocket leaves on each of 4 plates and arrange the mackerel slices and leeks on top. Spoon some of the sauce over the fish and serve with the remaining sauce on the side.

SIMMERED RED SNAPPER WITH SATOIMO

MEDAI NO NIMONO SATOIMO SOE

SERVES 4 PREPARATION TIME: 20 MINUTES COOKING TIME: 20 MINUTES

With its stunningly beautiful red skin and meaty flesh, red snapper is a dream fish. Cook the fish gently, steaming or simmering it, so you do not spoil the skin pattern, rather than using the more harsh cooking methods of grilling or pan-frying.

5cm/2in piece **root ginger**

7.5cm/3in piece **cucumber**, quartered lengthways, deseeded and cut into matchsticks

8 small **satoimo**, peeled, neatly trimmed and rinsed in water to remove starch

2 tbsp **mirin**

½ tsp **sea salt**

1 large **red snapper**, about 700g/1lb 9oz total weight, filleted and halved crossways

4 red **shiso** sprigs (optional)

COOKING SAUCE:

125ml/4fl oz/½ cup **saké**

125ml/4fl oz/½ cup **mirin**

150ml/5fl oz/scant ⅔ cup **shoyu**

1 CUT the ginger in half and slice one half thinly. Peel the other half and cut into very thin matchsticks; cover with cold water to freshen up. Drain and pat dry with kitchen paper then mix with the cucumber.

2 PUT the satoimo in a small saucepan, cover with cold water and bring to the boil. Reduce the heat and simmer for 3–4 minutes until cooked through but still firm, then drain. Put 250ml/9fl oz/1 cup water in the saucepan, add the mirin and salt and bring to the boil. Return the satoimo to the pan, reduce the heat to low, then simmer gently for 2–3 minutes. Drain and set aside.

3 MAKE the cooking sauce by mixing the saké, mirin and shoyu with 250ml/9fl oz/1 cup water. Pour into a saucepan and bring to the boil. Add the sliced ginger and the red snapper, then cover and simmer over a medium heat for about 10 minutes or until the sauce thickens.

4 PLACE a slice of fish on each of 4 plates, pour some of the sauce over and arrange 2 satoimo beside the fish. Serve with the red shiso, if using, the ginger and the cucumber matchsticks.

SWORDFISH TERIYAKI WITH CELERY

KAJIKI-MAGURO NO TERIYAKI

SERVES 4   PREPARATION TIME: 15 MINUTES, PLUS 10 MINUTES MARINATING
COOKING TIME: 20 MINUTES

Teriyaki *(meaning "glow-grill") is a method of marinating and grilling fish or meat that gives it a golden hue. Salmon, chicken or beef are also very good for teriyaki.*

4 **swordfish** steaks, about 200g/7oz each

1 tbsp **vegetable oil**, plus extra for oiling

6 **celery** sticks, cut diagonally into 1cm/½in thick slices

a splash **shoyu**

a pinch powdered **sansho** (optional)

sea **salt** and freshly ground **black pepper**

TERIYAKI SAUCE:

100ml/3½fl oz/scant ½ cup **shoyu**

185ml/6fl oz/¾ cup **mirin**

185ml/6fl oz/¾ cup **saké**

1 MAKE the teriyaki sauce by putting the shoyu, mirin and saké in a shallow dish and mixing well. Add the swordfish, spoon the marinade over the top and leave to marinate for 10 minutes.

2 HEAT a non-stick frying pan, add the oil and celery and stir-fry for 3–4 minutes until just tender. Season lightly with salt, pepper and shoyu. Remove the celery from the pan and keep warm.

3 WIPE the frying pan with oiled kitchen paper and add 2 swordfish steaks. Fry over a medium heat for 2–3 minutes until golden, then turn and spoon 4 tbsp of the teriyaki sauce over the fish. Fry for a further 2–3 minutes until golden, then continue to cook, turning frequently, for a further 1–2 minutes. Remove from the pan and set aside. Wipe the pan with the same oiled kitchen paper, then cook the remaining 2 swordfish steaks in the same way.

4 ARRANGE some of the celery in the centre of each of 4 plates and place a swordfish steak on top. Spoon some more teriyaki sauce over the steaks, sprinkle with a little powdered sansho, if using, and serve.

SEA BASS MARINATED IN MISO AND GRILLED *SUSUZI NO MISO-YAKI*

SERVES 4   PREPARATION TIME: 25 MINUTES, PLUS 3—7 DAYS MARINATING AND 20 MINUTES SALTING   COOKING TIME: 15 MINUTES

Made famous at Japanese restaurants in the West using normally rarely available black cod, miso-yaki (miso-grill) is one of the ancient techniques of Japanese cooking that still thrives to this day. Use any oily fish, such as salmon and sea bass.

2 large **sea bass**, about 1.25kg/2lb 12oz total weight, filleted and each cut crossways into 3 pieces

1 tsp **sea salt**

4 **pickled daikon chrysanthemums** (*see page 20*) (**optional**)

MISO MARINADE:

600g/1lb 5oz **white miso**

125g/4oz **khaki miso**

6 tbsp **saké**

6 tbsp **mirin**

1 **SPRINKLE** the sea bass with the salt and leave for 20 minutes. Pat dry with kitchen paper.

2 **MAKE** the miso marinade by mixing together the white miso, khaki miso, saké and mirin. Spread a third of the marinade in a shallow container that is large enough to hold 2 sea bass fillets in a single layer. Cover the marinade with a muslin cloth, then place half the fillets flat on the cloth and cover with another muslin cloth. Spread half of the remaining miso marinade on top, cover with another muslin cloth and top with the remaining fillets. Cover with another muslin cloth and spread the remaining miso marinade on top. Finally, cover with a lid and leave to marinate in the fridge for a minimum of 3 days and up to 7 days.

3 **HEAT** the grill to medium. Remove the sea bass from the marinade and muslin and grill for 4—5 minutes on each side until golden.

4 **ARRANGE** pieces of the sea bass on each of 4 plates, add a pickled daikon chrysanthemum, if using, then serve.

SALMON HOTPOT

ISHIKARI NABE

**SERVES 4   PREPARATION TIME: 20 MINUTES, PLUS 10 MINUTES SALTING
COOKING TIME: 20 MINUTES**

*This is a hearty family hotpot, good for a shivering winter's night. You can use cod
or haddock instead of salmon and any other vegetables you like, making this dish
a good way to use up leftovers in the fridge.*

3 **salmon** steaks, about 450g/1lb total weight,
  cut into large bite-sized pieces

sea salt, for sprinkling

2 **carrots**, peeled and cut into bite-sized pieces

2 **turnips**, cut into bite-sized pieces

4–5 tbsp **khaki miso**

1 tsp **dashi** granules

2 **leeks**, sliced diagonally into 2.5cm/1in
  thick pieces

8 **shiitake mushrooms**, stems trimmed

1 block **firm tofu**, about 300g/10½oz, cut into
  bite-sized cubes

30g/1oz **mangetout**, trimmed

seven-spice chilli powder, for sprinkling
  (optional)

1 **SPRINKLE** the salmon with salt and set aside for 10 minutes.

2 **PUT** the carrots and turnips in a large casserole, half fill with water
(about 450ml/16fl oz/scant 2 cups) and bring to the boil. Lower the heat
and simmer over a medium heat for 3 minutes.

3 **ADD** the salmon and continue to cook, skimming off the foam that
forms on the surface.

4 **DILUTE** the miso with some of the cooking liquid, then stir it into the
casserole. Add the dashi granules and check the seasoning.

5 **ADD** the leeks, shiitake and tofu and continue to simmer for 2 minutes.
Finally, add the mangetout and cook for a further 1 minute.

6 **DIVIDE** the salmon and vegetables between 4 soup bowls and serve
hot, sprinkled with a little seven-spice chilli powder, if using.

MONKFISH SHABU-SHABU *ANKOU NABE*

SERVES 4   PREPARATION TIME: 25 MINUTES   COOKING TIME: 10 MINUTES

Monkfish is synonymous with winter in Japan, and there is no better way to taste the season than by cooking and eating it in a good hotpot with family and friends.

1 **monkfish** tail, about 650g/1½lb total weight, bones reserved, sliced crossways into 1cm/½in pieces

1 block **firm tofu**, about 300g/10½oz, cut into 2.5cm/1in cubes

200g/7oz packet **shirataki**

8 **Chinese leaves**, cut into 5cm/2in squares

250g/9oz **spinach**, tough stalks discarded

1 bunch **enoki mushrooms**, trimmed

8 **shiitake mushrooms**, stems trimmed

4 **eryngii mushrooms** (optional)

20cm/8in piece dried **konbu**

PONZU SAUCE:

juice of 1 **lemon**

juice of 1 **lime**

7 tbsp **shoyu**

1 tbsp **mirin**

pinch of **dashi** granules mixed in 2 tbsp hot water

1 tbsp **saké**

1 **ARRANGE** the monkfish on a serving plate with the tofu and shirataki.

2 **PLACE** the Chinese leaves on one corner of a second serving plate and arrange the spinach and mushrooms next to them.

3 **PUT** the konbu and plenty of water in a large casserole with the bones from the fish, then bring to the boil. Remove and discard the konbu, then simmer over a medium heat for 5 minutes. Remove the bones and transfer the casserole to a gas ring or electric hotplate placed on the dining table.

4 **MAKE** the ponzu sauce by putting the lemon and lime juice, shoyu, mirin, dashi granules and saké in a bowl and mixing well. Pour the sauce into 4 small dishes.

5 **ARRANGE** the fish and vegetable plates on the table and put some of each ingredient into the casserole. Skim the froth from the surface with a spoon and adjust the heat during cooking so the water is gently simmering. When the fish and vegetables are cooked, diners help themselves, dipping the individual pieces into the ponzu sauce.

6 **ADD** more fish and vegetables to the casserole as necessary. After all the ingredients are cooked, use the stock to cook leftover rice or noodles.

TEMPURA *TEMPURA*

SERVES 4 PREPARATION TIME: 35 MINUTES COOKING TIME: 30 MINUTES

The key to the success of tempura lies in a golden, crisp batter and timing. For a light batter, even the flour should be chilled (ideally overnight), and tempura should be eaten immediately after frying.

8 raw large **king prawns**, heads and shells removed but tails kept intact, deveined (*see page 19*)

1 **green pepper**, quartered, deseeded and each quarter halved crossways

1 small **carrot**, peeled, halved crossways and each half quartered lengthways

4 **shiitake mushrooms**, stalks trimmed

vegetable oil, for deep-frying

7.5cm/3in piece **daikon**, peeled and grated

2.5cm/1in piece **root ginger**, peeled and grated

BATTER:

2 **egg yolks**, beaten

300g/10½oz/2⅓ cups **plain flour**, sifted and refrigerated overnight, plus extra for dusting

DIPPING SAUCE:

350ml/12fl oz/scant 1½ cups **Dashi** (*see page 27*)

5 tbsp **shoyu**

5 tbsp **mirin**

1 **MAKE** the dipping sauce by mixing the dashi, shoyu and mirin in a saucepan. Bring to the boil, then remove from the heat and set aside.

2 **CUT** several slits along the belly of each prawn to stop it curling when heated. Dust the prawns, pepper and carrot with plain flour and shake off the excess. Dust the caps of the shiitake in flour. Heat the oil in a deep-fryer or wok to about 170°C/340°F.

3 **MAKE** the batter by mixing 450ml/16fl oz/scant 2 cups ice-cold water into the egg yolks and sifting in the chilled flour. Using a fork, lightly fold several times – do not stir, as the batter should still be lumpy.

4 **DIP** the pepper and carrot pieces into the batter, then gently slide them, one by one, into the hot oil. Fry for 1–2 minutes until light golden, then remove using a slotted spoon and drain on a wire rack. Dip the back of the shiitake caps into the batter, then fry in the hot oil for 1–2 minutes.

5 **DIP** each prawn in the batter, holding it by the tail, then slowly slide them into the hot oil. Fry 4 prawns at a time for 2–3 minutes until light golden, then remove using a slotted spoon and drain.

6 **ARRANGE** the tempura on 4 plates with a small mound of daikon and ginger. Serve immediately with the reheated dipping sauce.

CAULIFLOWER AND EDAMAME WITH WASABI DRESSING

KARIFURAWA TO EDAMAME NO WASABI-AE

SERVES 4 PREPARATION TIME: 15 MINUTES, PLUS 10 MINUTES MARINATING
COOKING TIME: 10 MINUTES

Vibrant green edamame (fresh soya beans in pods) are now increasingly available outside Japan. If you cannot find them, however, use either frozen soya beans or green peas instead for this very easy, but delicious and beautiful, dish.

1 small **cauliflower**, about 300g/10½oz, separated into small florets and stems cut into similar-sized pieces

sea salt

300g/10½oz **edamame** pods or about 120g/4¼oz shelled beans

4 **iceberg lettuce** leaves

WASABI DRESSING:

2 tbsp **mayonnaise**

¾ tsp **wasabi** paste

2 tbsp **lemon** juice

1 tsp **sugar**

1 BOIL the cauliflower florets and stem pieces in lightly salted boiling water over a high heat for 3 minutes until just tender. Drain and place under cold running water to cool quickly. Pat dry with kitchen paper and set aside.

2 BOIL the edamame in their pods in highly salted boiling water over a high heat for 4–5 minutes until tender. Drain and place under cold running water to cool quickly. Remove the beans from their pods. (If using shelled edamame, boil in lightly salted boiling water for 3 minutes, drain and place under cold running water to cool quickly. Pat dry with kitchen paper.)

3 MAKE the wasabi dressing by mixing the mayonnaise, wasabi, lemon juice and sugar in a salad bowl until smooth. Add the cauliflower, toss lightly in the dressing and leave to marinate for 10 minutes.

4 ADD the edamame and mix gently. Put a lettuce leaf on each of 4 plates and spoon the salad on top.

GREEN BEANS WITH WHITE DRESSING

NINJIN TO SAYAINGEN NO SHIRA-AE

SERVES 4   PREPARATION TIME: 15 MINUTES   COOKING TIME: 8 MINUTES

Tofu's versatility and nutritious qualities can be appreciated in various forms. This tofu dressing adds depth as well as a rich flavour to the vegetables. Use any vegetable or a combination of your choice.

300g/10½oz **green beans**, trimmed and sliced diagonally into 5cm/2in pieces

1 **carrot**, peeled and cut into 5cm/2in strips

1 tbsp **black sesame seeds**

WHITE DRESSING:

½ block **firm tofu**, about 150g/5½oz, broken into 4–5 pieces

1 tbsp **tahini** (sesame seed paste)

2 tsp **sugar**

1–2 drops **shoyu**

sea salt

1–2 tbsp **soya milk** or **water**

1 COOK the beans in lightly salted boiling water over a high heat for 3–4 minutes until just tender. Drain and place under cold running water to cool quickly. Pat dry with kitchen paper and set aside. Repeat with the carrot.

2 MAKE the white dressing. Put the tofu in a pan of boiling water and bring back to the boil. Remove from the heat and drain in a colander lined with muslin or a clean tea towel. Leave the tofu to cool, then wrap it in the cloth and squeeze out excess water. Unwrap the tofu and put it in a mixing bowl.

3 ADD the tahini to the tofu and mix to form a smooth paste, pressing with the back of a spoon. Add the sugar, shoyu and salt to taste, then add the soya milk, a little at a time, and mix to make a slightly runny dressing. Check the seasoning, adding more shoyu or salt if necessary.

4 PUT the green beans and carrot in a large mixing bowl, spoon over the dressing and mix lightly. Arrange in a shallow salad bowl, sprinkle with black sesame seeds and serve.

ASPARAGUS WITH SESAME DRESSING

ASUPARAGASU NO GOMA-AÉ

SERVES 4   PREPARATION TIME: 15 MINUTES   COOKING TIME: 10 MINUTES

Goma-aé (sweet sesame dressing) is regularly used by the Japanese to dress-up plainly cooked vegetables. Here, harusame vermicelli, if you choose to use them, also get coated in the dressing.

24–28 **asparagus** spears, halved

shoyu, to taste

125g/4oz dried **harusame vermicelli** (*see page 11*), soaked in water for 10 minutes (optional)

2 tbsp **lemon** juice

1 tbsp **olive oil**

sea salt and freshly ground **black pepper**

SWEET SESAME DRESSING:

5 tbsp **white sesame seeds**, lightly toasted

2 tbsp **sugar**

2 tbsp **saké**

1 **COOK** the asparagus in lightly salted boiling water for 4–5 minutes until just tender. Drain and place under cold running water to cool quickly. Pat dry with kitchen paper, sprinkle with a little shoyu and set aside.

2 **DRAIN** the vermicelli, if using, and cook in boiling water over a medium heat for 6–7 minutes until soft. Drain and place under cold running water to cool quickly and drain well again. Roughly pat dry with kitchen paper, put in a mixing bowl and stir in the lemon juice, olive oil and salt and pepper to taste.

3 **MAKE** the sweet sesame dressing by grinding the sesame seeds in a Japanese grinder and pestle (see page 23) or electric grinder until roughly half of the seeds are crushed. Add the sugar, saké and a pinch of salt and mix together.

4 **STIR** 2 tbsp of the sesame dressing into the vermicelli until evenly coated.

5 **ADD** the cooked asparagus to the remaining sesame dressing and mix gently until evenly coated. Arrange the dressed asparagus on a bed of vermicelli and serve.

BROCCOLI SALAD WITH ANCHOVY SANBAIZU DRESSING

BUROKKORI NO ANCHOBI SANBAIZU-AE

SERVES 4   PREPARATION TIME: 10 MINUTES   COOKING TIME: 7 MINUTES

Sanbaizu (meaning "three parts vinegar") is a traditional Japanese salad dressing comprising sugar, shoyu and rice vinegar. Anchovies are added to this version to add extra depth as well as to reduce the sweetness, although vegetarians can omit them.

300g/10½oz **broccoli**, cut into small florets

1 bunch **watercress**, broken into small sprigs

1 tsp **sesame oil**

ANCHOVY SANBAIZU DRESSING:

3 salted **anchovy** fillets

1 tbsp **sugar**

2 tbsp **rice vinegar**

2 tbsp **shoyu**

1 COOK the broccoli in lightly salted boiling water over a medium heat for about 5 minutes until just tender. Drain and place under cold running water to cool quickly. Pat dry with kitchen paper and set aside.

2 MAKE the anchovy sanbaizu dressing by putting the anchovy fillets in a Japanese grinder and pestle (see page 23) or in a food processor and pounding or processing to a smooth paste. Add the sugar, rice vinegar and shoyu and stir well until the sugar dissolves.

3 PUT the broccoli and watercress in a mixing bowl, pour over the dressing and drizzle with the sesame oil. Toss gently to coat the salad evenly in the dressing.

4 DIVIDE the salad between 4 plates and serve.

ENOKI, CUCUMBER AND CELERY SALAD WITH VINAIGRETTE *ENOKI NO SUNOMONO*

SERVES 4   PREPARATION TIME: 15 MINUTES, PLUS 10 MINUTES MARINATING

Typically made with cucumber and wakame seaweed, this sunomono (rice vinegar-dressed salad) uses uncooked enoki and crisp celery to give it a wonderfully fresh crunchiness.

½ **cucumber**, quartered lengthways, deseeded and sliced diagonally into 5cm/2in long strips

2 tsp **sea salt**

2 **celery** sticks, sliced diagonally into 5cm/2in long strips

1 bunch **enoki mushrooms**, trimmed and stalks separated

1–2 tsp **sesame oil**

2.5cm/1in piece **root ginger**, peeled and cut into thin matchsticks

VINAIGRETTE:

5 tbsp **rice vinegar**

1 tbsp **sugar**

1 tbsp **saké**

1 tbsp **mirin**

½ tbsp **shoyu**

1 SPRINKLE the cucumber with 1 tsp salt. Press the cucumber with your hands a few times, then squeeze out the excess water. Transfer to a mixing bowl. Repeat with the celery, using the remaining salt.

2 ADD the enoki to the cucumber and celery and mix gently.

3 FRESHEN up the ginger in cold water for a minute or so, then drain and pat dry with kitchen paper.

4 MAKE the vinaigrette by putting the vinegar, sugar, saké, mirin and shoyu in a small mixing bowl and stirring well until the sugar dissolves. Pour the dressing over the vegetables, toss gently and leave to marinate for 5 minutes until the enoki wilts slightly. Sprinkle over a little sesame oil and mix gently again.

5 DIVIDE the salad between 4 dishes, add the ginger and serve.

SIMMERED SOYA BEANS

DAIZU NO GOMOKU-NI

SERVES 4   PREPARATION TIME: 15 MINUTES, PLUS 8 HOURS SOAKING
COOKING TIME: 2 HOURS

The delicate heartiness of daizu (soya beans) is best appreciated by simply simmering them with umami-rich konbu, as in this traditional home-cooked recipe.

150g/5½oz/¾ cup dried **soya beans**, rinsed and soaked overnight in cold water

5cm/2in square piece dried **konbu**, cut into 8mm/⅓in square pieces

3 tbsp **sugar**

2 tbsp **shoyu**

1 **carrot**, peeled and cut into 1cm/¼in cubes

½ slab **konnyaku**, about 125g/4½oz, cut into 1cm/½in cubes (optional)

1 RUB the beans between your hands and discard the transparent skin that surrounds them. Put the beans in a saucepan, add roughly three times as much water as the beans and bring to the boil over a high heat. When froth starts to rise to the surface, remove the pan from the heat and drain. Rinse the beans to remove the froth.

2 PUT the beans back into the saucepan, add the konbu and 850ml/29fl oz/scant 3½ cups water and bring to the boil over a high heat. Lower the heat and simmer very gently, half-covered, for about 1 hour until the soya beans are tender.

3 SEASON the beans with the sugar and shoyu, then stir and continue to simmer, still covered, for 30 minutes. Add the carrot and konnyaku, if using, mix gently together and continue to simmer for a further 30 minutes.

4 TIP the beans into a deep serving bowl and serve hot or cold.

SIMMERED ASSORTED VEGETABLES

YASAI NO NISHIME

SERVES 4 PREPARATION TIME: 20 MINUTES, PLUS 30 MINUTES SOAKING
COOKING TIME: 25 MINUTES

Simple, unadulterated food is the essence of Japanese cooking, and there is no better example of this than these simple simmered vegetables in a sweet shoyu sauce. For vegetarians, use the shiitake soaking liquid in place of dashi, adding water to make it up to the same amount.

1 slab **konnyaku**, about 250g/9oz (optional)

40g/1½oz **mangetout**, trimmed

10 x 30cm/4 x 12in piece dried **konbu**

2 **carrots**, peeled and sliced into thin rounds

2 **turnips**, each cut into 6 wedges

8 dried **shiitake mushrooms**, soaked in warm water for 30 minutes, drained and stems removed

COOKING SAUCE:

1 litre/35fl oz/4 cups **Dashi** (*see page 27*)

4 tbsp **shoyu**

3 tbsp **sugar**

4 tbsp **mirin**

4 tbsp **saké**

1 **SLICE** the konnyaku, if using, crossways into 5mm/¼in thick rectangular pieces and make a cut, about 3cm/1¼in long, lengthways in the centre of each piece. Fold one end through the cut to make a twist.

2 **BOIL** the mangetout in lightly salted boiling water over a medium heat for 1 minute. Drain and place under cold running water to cool quickly, then set aside.

3 **MOISTEN** the konbu with wet kitchen paper, cut into eight 2.5 x 15cm/1 x 6in ribbons and knot each ribbon in the centre.

4 **MAKE** the cooking sauce by mixing the dashi, shoyu, sugar, mirin and saké in a saucepan and stirring until the sugar dissolves. Add the carrots, turnips, konnyaku, shiitake and konbu and bring to the boil over a high heat, skimming off the foam on the surface.

5 **REDUCE** the heat, cover and simmer gently over a medium heat for 12–15 minutes until the sauce has reduced by two-thirds; leave to cool.

6 **ARRANGE** the cooked vegetables in 4 deep bowls and serve.

TOFU SALAD WITH UMEBOSHI DRESSING

HIYA-YAKKO SALADA UMEBOSHI AE

SERVES 4   PREPARATION TIME: 10 MINUTES, PLUS 10 MINUTES SOAKING

Perfect for a hot summer's day, this refreshing yet nutritious dish is quick to prepare. Umeboshi (dried and pickled Japanese plums) are good for digestion and are available at Japanese supermarkets.

2 tbsp dried **wakame**, soaked in water for 10 minutes

1 **spring onion**, cut into 5cm/2in thin strips

2 blocks **firm tofu**, about 700g/1lb 9oz, cut into 2.5cm/1in cubes

2 large **tomatoes**, peeled, deseeded and chopped into bite-sized pieces

sea salt and freshly ground **black pepper**

4 large **lettuce** leaves, to serve

UMEBOSHI DRESSING:

2 large **dried and pickled plums**, pitted

2 tbsp **shoyu**

2 tbsp **rice vinegar**

1 DRAIN the wakame and squeeze out the excess water. Pat dry with kitchen paper, sprinkle with a little salt and pepper and toss lightly.

2 COVER the spring onion strips in cold water for a minute or so, then drain and pat dry with kitchen paper.

3 MAKE the dressing by putting the dried and pickled plums in a Japanese grinder and pestle (see page 23) or in a food processor and grind or process until they form a smooth paste. Mix in the shoyu, rice vinegar and salt and pepper to taste.

4 MIX the tofu, tomatoes and wakame in a mixing bowl, pour over the dressing and toss gently.

5 PLACE a lettuce leaf in the centre of each of 4 bowls and top with the tofu salad. Serve sprinkled with the spring onion strips.

PAK CHOI AND BABY CLAMS IN MUSTARD DRESSING *PAKUCHOI TO ASARI NO KARASHI-AE*

SERVES 4　PREPARATION TIME: 10 MINUTES　COOKING TIME: 5 MINUTES

Traditionally, spinach is used for this recipe, but Western spinach has a softer texture and is less flavoursome than oriental varieties, so pak choi is used here instead – and the result is a delicious, crunchy, lemony salad.

300g/10½oz **pak choi**

sea salt

100g/3½oz canned **baby clams**

MUSTARD DRESSING:

2 tsp **English mustard**

2 tbsp **lemon** juice

1 tbsp **shoyu**

2 tbsp **brine** from the baby clams

1 **BOIL** the pak choi in lightly salted boiling water over a medium heat for 2 minutes until tender. Drain and place under cold running water to cool quickly. Squeeze out the excess water, then cut off the stems. Cut the leaves into 4cm/1½in slices, then cut the broad white part of the leaves in half, if large.

2 **DRAIN** the baby clams, retaining 2 tbsp of the brine, and put them in a mixing bowl with the pak choi.

3 **MAKE** the mustard dressing by putting the mustard, lemon juice, shoyu and brine from the clams in a bowl and stirring well until smooth. Pour the dressing over the pak choi and clams and toss gently.

4 **ARRANGE** the salad on 4 plates and serve.

RICE BOWL WITH MINCED CHICKEN AND SCRAMBLED EGG *SOBORO DONBURI*

SERVES 4 PREPARATION TIME: 15 MINUTES, PLUS 30 MINUTES SOAKING COOKING TIME: 20 MINUTES

Soboro *is the term used to describe food that is flaky in texture, such as this minced chicken and scrambled egg dish. This dish can also be arranged in a lunchbox and taken to school or work.*

---

3 tbsp **vegetable oil**

500g/1lb 2oz **minced chicken**

2.5cm/1in piece **root ginger**, grated and juice squeezed out

3 tbsp **saké**

6 tbsp **shoyu**

2 tbsp **sugar**

3 **eggs**, beaten

¾ tsp **sea salt**

40g/1½oz **mangetout**, trimmed

2 recipe quantities **Plain Boiled Japanese Rice** (*see page 24*)

4 **pickled radish flowers** (*see page 20*) (optional)

1 **HEAT** 2 tbsp of the oil in a frying pan and cook the chicken with the ginger juice, saké, shoyu and 1 tbsp each of sugar and water. Cook for 4–5 minutes, stirring and crushing the chicken with the back of a fork as it cooks, until it turns pale and separates into fine granules. Remove from the heat and set aside.

2 **MIX** together the eggs, salt and the rest of the sugar. Heat the remaining oil in a clean frying pan and add the egg mixture. Stir gently and continuously until the eggs are scrambled into very fine granules. Remove from the heat and set aside.

3 **COOK** the mangetout in lightly salted boiling water for 1 minute, then drain and place under cold running water to cool quickly. Pat dry with kitchen paper, then cut into thin strips.

4 **DIVIDE** the cooked rice between 4 deep bowls. Cover one half of the rice in each bowl with a quarter of the chicken mixture and the other half with a quarter of the egg. Arrange the mangetout in a line between them, add a pickled radish flower, if using, and serve.

RICE BOWL WITH CHICKEN AND EGG

OYAKO DONBURI

SERVES **4**   PREPARATION TIME: **15** MINUTES   COOKING TIME: **25** MINUTES

This popular lunch dish is called oyako *(meaning "parent and child"), signifying the two main ingredients, chicken and egg. Make it in individual servings using a small frying pan. The egg should be slightly runny so that it penetrates the rice below.*

1½ recipe quantities **Plain Boiled Japanese Rice** *(see page 24),* kept warm

4 boneless **chicken thighs**, about 350g/12oz, skinned and sliced diagonally into thin, bite-sized pieces

1 **onion**, halved and cut into half-moons

150g/5½oz **rocket** leaves

4 **eggs**, beaten

COOKING SAUCE:

250ml/9fl oz/1 cup **Dashi** *(see page 27)*

7 tbsp **shoyu**

2 tbsp **sugar**

4 tbsp **saké**

4 tbsp **mirin**

1 MAKE the cooking sauce by mixing the dashi, shoyu, sugar, saké and mirin in a saucepan. Bring to the boil over a high heat, stirring until the sugar dissolves, then remove the pan from the heat.

2 DIVIDE the rice between 4 bowls and cover with a lid or a small plate to keep it warm.

3 PUT a quarter of the cooking sauce in a pancake pan or small frying pan, about 15cm/6in in diameter, and bring to the boil. Add a quarter of the chicken and onion and cook over a medium heat for 3–4 minutes, stirring, until the chicken turns pale.

4 ADD a quarter of the rocket to the pan and pour 1 beaten egg evenly over the top. Cover with a lid and continue to cook, gently shaking the pan, for about 30 seconds. Do not overcook – it should still be loose with some juice.

5 REMOVE from the heat and slide the mixture on top of a serving of rice. Place a lid on to keep warm while you cook the remaining 3 portions of chicken, rocket and egg in the same way.

RICE COOKED WITH CHESTNUTS

KURI GOHAN

SERVES 4   PREPARATION TIME: 15 MINUTES, PLUS 30 MINUTES SOAKING
COOKING TIME: 15 MINUTES

Chestnuts represent autumn, and as soon as they appear in the shops, so does this dish on Japanese tables. You can use ordinary rice, but the addition of glutinous rice gives the dish extra weight and texture.

175g/6oz/heaped ¾ cup **Japanese short grain rice**

70g/2½oz/⅓ cup **glutinous rice**

5cm/2in square piece dried **konbu** (optional)

5–6 fresh **chestnuts**

2 tbsp **saké**

½ tsp **sea salt**

sesame seeds, toasted

1 **PUT** both types of rice in a bowl and mix well. Wash thoroughly, changing the water several times until it is clear, then drain. Transfer the rice to a heavy-based saucepan, approximately 14cm/5½in in diameter. Add 350ml/12fl oz/scant 1½ cups water and the konbu, if using, then leave for 30 minutes.

2 **COOK** the chestnuts in boiling water for 10 minutes, then drain and peel and cut each one into 2–3 bite-sized pieces.

3 **MIX** the saké and salt into the rice and put the chestnuts on top. Cover the saucepan with a lid and bring to the boil over a medium heat. Lower the heat to minimum and simmer for 12 minutes until the water has been absorbed but bubbles are still forming on top of the rice.

4 **REMOVE** and discard the konbu. Lightly turn the rice from bottom to top with a wooden spatula, then continue to simmer, covered, for another minute. Remove the pan from the heat and leave to stand, still covered, for 10 minutes.

5 **TURN** the rice gently from bottom to top so that the chestnuts are evenly spread. Serve hot in rice bowls, sprinkled with sesame seeds.

BEETROOT SOUP RICE WITH JAPANESE MUSHROOMS *KINOKO IRI BITSU ZOUSUI*

SERVES 4   PREPARATION TIME: 15 MINUTES   COOKING TIME: 20 MINUTES

This traditional, earthy dish, normally cooked with plain dashi soup, becomes beautiful and interesting with the addition of fresh beetroot. Zousui (soup rice) is a good way to use up cold, leftover rice.

1 uncooked **beetroot**

1 tsp **dashi** granules

1–2 tsp **sea salt**

3 tbsp **shoyu**

70g/2½oz **shimeji mushrooms**, trimmed and stalks separated

4 **shiitake mushrooms**, trimmed and cut into thin strips

60g/2¼oz **enoki mushrooms**, trimmed and separated into small bunches

1 recipe quantity warm or cold **Plain Boiled Japanese Rice** *(see page 24)*

a squeeze of **lemon** juice

1 **spring onion**, finely shredded

1 **CUT** off the root end of the beetroot, then peel carefully and cut into matchsticks. Put in a saucepan with 1.25 litres/44fl oz/5 cups water and bring to the boil over a high heat. Lower the heat and simmer gently for about 15 minutes until cooked. Add the dashi granules and season to taste with the salt and shoyu.

2 **ADD** the shimeji to the pan, bring back to the boil and simmer over a medium heat for 1 minute. Add the shiitake and simmer for a further 1 minute. Add the enoki and simmer for another minute, then remove the pan from the heat.

3 **DIVIDE** the warm rice, if using, between 4 bowls and pour the soup over. Place the mushrooms on top, then add the lemon juice and serve hot, sprinkled with the spring onion shreds. If using cold rice, add it to the soup to heat through thoroughly before arranging in bowls and serving as above.

SOUP RAMEN WITH SHREDDED BEEF

GYUNIKU NO SENGIRI IRI RAMEN

SERVES 4   PREPARATION TIME: 20 MINUTES   COOKING TIME: 20 MINUTES

Japanese ramen have become phenomenally popular all over the world following in the footsteps of sushi, and, just like sushi, they come with enormous varieties of toppings. The meat and vegetables are cut thinly for this recipe.

400g/14oz dried **ramen noodles**

350g/12oz sirloin or rump **beef**, half-frozen to make slicing easier

1.5 litres/52fl oz/6 cups **chicken stock**

2.5cm/1in piece **root ginger**, roughly sliced

2 **garlic** cloves, halved

2 tbsp **saké**

150ml/5fl oz/⅔ cup **shoyu**, plus 1 tbsp for stir-frying

1 **pak choi**, trimmed and thinly shredded

2 tbsp **vegetable oil**

8 dried **shiitake mushrooms**, soaked in warm water for 30 minutes, drained and thinly sliced

sea salt and freshly ground **black pepper**

1 **COOK** the ramen noodles following the instructions on the packet, then drain. Rinse the noodles to remove the starch, then drain in a fine-mesh colander and set aside.

2 **CUT** the beef into thin strips and leave to thaw completely while preparing the remaining ingredients.

3 **HEAT** the chicken stock in a saucepan, add the ginger and garlic and simmer gently over a medium heat for 10 minutes. Remove the flavourings using a slotted spoon and discard. Season the broth with the saké, shoyu and salt and pepper, to taste, then remove from the heat.

4 **STIR-FRY** the pak choi in 1 tbsp of the oil in a frying pan or wok over a medium heat for 1–2 minutes, then transfer to a plate. Add the remaining oil to the pan and stir-fry the shiitake and beef over a medium heat for 2–3 minutes until the meat turns pale. Season with 1 tbsp of the shoyu, and salt and pepper and remove from the heat.

5 **POUR** boiling water over the cooked noodles to warm them, then drain them and divide between 4 bowls. Spoon the soup over the noodles and top with the beef, shiitake and pak choi. Serve hot.

SOBA NOODLES WITH TEMPURA
TEMPURA SOBA

SERVES **4**   PREPARATION TIME: **20** MINUTES   COOKING TIME: **30** MINUTES

Soba noodles can be eaten hot in dashi soup or cold dipped in a sauce. The plain, light soba and crisp, golden tempura featured here are a surprising match, and this dish is one of the regular items at soba restaurants.

400g/14oz dried **soba noodles**

150g/5oz raw peeled **prawns**

1 small **carrot**, peeled and cut into matchsticks

1 small **parsnip**, peeled and cut into matchsticks

60g/2¼oz **fine beans**, trimmed and cut into matchsticks

150g/5½oz/1¼ cups **plain flour**, sifted and chilled

vegetable oil, for deep-frying

BROTH:

1.25 litres/44fl oz/5 cups **Dashi** *(see page 27)*

1 tsp **sea salt**

1 tbsp **sugar**

125ml/4fl oz/½ cup **shoyu**

1 COOK the soba noodles following the instructions on the packet, then drain. Rinse the noodles to remove the starch then drain in a fine-mesh colander and set aside.

2 PUT the prawns and vegetables in a mixing bowl, sprinkle with a little of the flour and mix well. Sift the remaining flour into 250ml/9fl oz/1 cup ice-cold water and, using a fork, lightly fold several times – do not stir. Add the prawns and vegetables and mix gently.

3 HEAT the vegetable oil to 170°C/340°F in a deep frying pan or wok.

4 SCOOP a quarter of the prawn and vegetable mixture into a ladle and gently slide into the hot oil. Fry for 3–4 minutes, turning once or twice, until crisp and light golden. Remove using a slotted spoon and drain on a wire rack. Repeat 3 more times.

5 PUT the ingredients for the broth in a saucepan and bring to the boil, stirring until the sugar dissolves. Add the soba noodles and heat through. Divide the soba and broth between 4 bowls and arrange the tempura on top of each serving. Serve hot.

FRIED RAMEN WITH MIXED SEAFOOD

KAISEN YAKISOBA

SERVES 4   PREPARATION TIME: 15 MINUTES   COOKING TIME: 10 MINUTES

Noodles are for everyone and every occasion, but they are normally served for lunch or as a filling snack. This colourful dish has been created with children in mind when they need an extra injection of nourishment after a day at school.

400g/14oz dried **ramen noodles**

4 tbsp **vegetable oil**, plus extra for sprinkling

2.5cm/1in piece **root ginger**, peeled and finely chopped

1–2 **garlic** cloves, finely chopped

400g/14oz cooked **mixed seafood**

1 tbsp **saké**

200g/7oz **beansprouts**, trimmed

40g/1½oz **mangetout**, trimmed and halved diagonally

½ **red pepper**, finely shredded

1 tbsp **shoyu**

sea salt and freshly ground **black pepper**

2 **spring onions**, finely shredded

green nori flakes (optional)

1 **COOK** the ramen noodles following the instructions on the packet, then drain. Rinse the noodles to remove the starch, then drain in a fine-mesh colander. Pat dry with kitchen paper, sprinkle with a little vegetable oil and toss lightly.

2 **HEAT** a frying pan or wok, add half of the oil and stir-fry the ginger and garlic over a medium heat for 1 minute. Add the seafood, stir-fry over a high heat for 1–2 minutes, then sprinkle with the saké.

3 **ADD** the beansprouts, mangetout and red pepper and stir-fry for another 1–2 minutes. Season with salt and pepper and mix in the shoyu. Remove the pan from the heat and transfer the seafood and vegetables to a mixing bowl.

4 **HEAT** a clean frying pan or wok and add the remaining oil, then the cooked ramen and gently stir-fry over a medium heat for 1 minute. Add the cooked seafood and vegetable mixture with any cooking juices, mix gently and continue to stir-fry for another 1–2 minutes. Remove from the heat.

5 **DIVIDE** between 4 plates, sprinkle with the spring onions and the green nori flakes, if using, and serve immediately.

UDON NOODLES IN EGG BROTH

KAKITAMA UDON

SERVES 4   PREPARATION TIME: 15 MINUTES
COOKING TIME: 15 MINUTES

Udon noodles are soothing to the palate as well as filling to the stomach, and make a very popular quick lunch or late-night supper. Add any vegetables, seafood or meat you like to this simple but delicious noodle dish.

400g/14oz dried **udon noodles**

3 tbsp **cornflour**, mixed with 3 tbsp water to make a paste

4 **eggs**, beaten

cress

2.5 cm/1in piece **root ginger**, peeled and grated (optional)

BROTH:

1.25 litres/44fl oz/5 cups **Dashi** (*see page 27*)

1½ tsp **sea salt**

1 tbsp **sugar**

120ml/4fl oz/½ cup **shoyu**

1 **COOK** the udon noodles following the instructions on the packet, then drain. Rinse the noodles to remove the starch, then drain in a fine-mesh colander and set aside.

2 **MAKE** the broth by putting the dashi, salt, sugar and shoyu in a saucepan. Bring to the boil over a high heat, stirring until the sugar dissolves. Lower the heat and slowly pour in the cornflour mixture, stirring all the time. The broth should thicken slightly.

3 **ADD** the beaten eggs, slowly pouring them over the surface of the broth, and cook for 2–3 minutes over a medium heat until the egg rises to the surface. Remove from the heat.

4 **POUR** boiling water over the cooked noodles to warm them, then drain and divide between 4 bowls. Spoon the egg broth over the top and serve with some cress and a heap of grated ginger, if using, on top.

RICE BALLS WRAPPED IN SWEET AZUKI PASTE *OHAGI*

MAKES **8** CAKES   PREPARATION TIME: **25** MINUTES, PLUS **3** HOURS TO OVERNIGHT SOAKING   COOKING TIME: **1** HOUR

This is a festival cake, with the red colour of the beans signifying a happy occasion. You can buy ready-made án (sweet azuki paste), but it's very easy to make your own.

150g/5½oz/¾ cup **glutinous rice**

mitsuba sprigs (optional)

SWEET AZUKI PASTE:

120g/4¼oz/scant ⅔ cup dried **azuki beans**, soaked in water for 3–4 hours or overnight

120g/4¼oz/scant ⅔ cup **sugar**

a pinch **salt**

1 **COOK** the rice in 220ml/7fl oz/scant 1 cup water following the method on page 24. While the rice is warm, gently pound, using a wet pestle or a rolling pin, until roughly half the rice is crushed.

2 **DRAIN** the azuki beans, put them in a saucepan and cover with plenty of water, then bring to the boil. Cook for 3 minutes over a high heat, then drain. Return the beans to the pan, pour in 450ml/16fl oz/scant 2 cups water and return to the boil. Lower the heat, partially cover and simmer for 30–45 minutes. Add the sugar in two stages and a pinch of salt, stirring until dissolved, then simmer for another 10–15 minutes.

3 **MASH** the beans in the cooking liquid using a potato masher, with the saucepan still over a low heat, stirring all the time until all the liquid has evaporated and the beans form a smooth paste. Leave to cool.

4 **DIVIDE** the rice into 8 and shape into oval balls. Spread about 1 heaped tbsp of the azuki paste into a thin disk, about 7.5cm/3in in diameter, in the centre of a clean, damp cloth about 15cm/6in square. Put a rice ball in the middle of the paste, then, using the cloth to help, wrap the paste around the rice to cover it. Repeat with the remaining rice and paste.

5 **PLACE** 2 balls on each of 4 plates and add some mitsuba, if using.

HALF GONG PANCAKES

DORAYAKI

SERVES 4   PREPARATION TIME: 20 MINUTES, PLUS 3 HOURS TO OVERNIGHT
SOAKING   COOKING TIME: 15 MINUTES

Japanese cakes use a lot of án (sweet azuki paste). These round, gong-shaped pancakes, stuffed with án and folded, are really simple and fun to make

1 large **egg**, beaten

5 tbsp **sugar**

1¼ tsp clear **honey**

90g/3oz/⅔ cup **plain flour**, sifted

½ tsp **baking powder**

vegetable oil, for frying

1 recipe quantity **Sweet Azuki Paste**
(*see page 170*)

shiso leaves (optional)

1 MIX the egg, sugar and honey in a bowl and, using a hand whisk, beat until the sugar dissolves.

2 ADD the flour, a little at a time, and mix well with the whisk to make a smooth batter. Dissolve the baking powder in 5 tbsp water and stir slowly into the batter, then beat well.

3 HEAT a frying pan, about 20cm/8in in diameter, over a medium heat. Add a little oil and wipe it over the base with kitchen paper until evenly coated. Reduce the heat to the lowest setting and ladle 3 tbsp of the batter into the pan – the batter should spread into a circle about 8cm/3in in diameter. Repeat the ladling twice to cook 3 pancakes at a time.

4 COOK the pancakes 3 minutes, then turn them over and cook the other side about 2 minutes until both sides are golden. Transfer the pancakes to a plate and repeat until you have made 8 pancakes.

5 SPREAD 1 heaped tbsp of the sweet azuki paste in the centre of a pancake and fold in half to make a "half gong". Repeat with the remaining pancakes and paste to make 8 "half gongs". Arrange on shiso leaves, if using, and serve warm or cold.

FRUIT SALAD WITH GINGER KANTEN

SHOUGA KANTEN NO FURUTSU SALADA

SERVES 4   PREPARATION TIME: 10 MINUTES, PLUS 30 MINUTES SETTING
COOKING TIME: 15 MINUTES

Jelly made with kanten, a marine algae extract, is indescribably light and soothing in the mouth and contrasts well in colour and texture with the fresh fruit in this salad.

1 tbsp **sugar**

1 sachet (2g) powdered **kanten**

2.5cm/1in piece **root ginger**, grated and juice squeezed out

1 small **red apple**, cut into 8 wedges, cored (optional)

½ **green apple**, cut into 4–6 wedges, cored and sliced into fan-shaped pieces

1 small **sharon fruit**, cut into fan-shaped pieces

6 **strawberries**, hulled and halved

a handful **blueberries**

SYRUP:

250ml/9fl oz/1 cup **rosewater**

5 tbsp clear **honey**

1 HEAT 250ml/9fl oz/1 cup water in a saucepan over a medium heat, add the sugar and sprinkle in the kanten. Stir gently for 1 to 2 minutes until the sugar and kanten dissolve (do not allow the mixture to boil). Remove the pan from the heat.

2 MIX the ginger juice into the kanten water. Pour into a metal mould, about 12 x 7.5 x 5cm deep/5 x 3 x 2in and leave to cool and set, about 30 minutes.

3 HEAT the rosewater in a small saucepan over a medium heat and mix in the honey (do not allow the mixture to boil). Stir until slightly thickened, then remove from the heat, leave to cool and then chill.

4 PUT the red and green apples in salted water for 1 minute, then drain and pat dry with kitchen paper. Make a V-shaped incision in one half of each wedge of red apple, cutting to just below the skin. Peel away the skin to make 8 pairs of "rabbit's ears", if using.

5 TURN out the set ginger jelly from its mould and cut into 1–2cm/ ½–¾in cubes. Put in a bowl with the apple, sharon fruit and strawberries and pour the chilled rosewater syrup over.

6 DIVIDE the fruit salad between 4 bowls and sprinkle with blueberries.

DRAGON FRUIT WITH CRANBERRY
KANTEN *DORAGON FURUTSU NO KURANBERI KANTEN SOE*

**SERVES 4   PREPARATION TIME: 5 MINUTES, PLUS 30 MINUTES SETTING
COOKING TIME: 5 MINUTES**

*The tartness of cranberry and the sweetness of exotic dragon fruit combine in this
gorgeous, visually stunning dessert.*

250ml/9fl oz/1 cup **cranberry juice**

2 tbsp **sugar**

1 sachet (2g) powdered **kanten**

2 **dragon fruit**

8 seedless **green grapes**, halved

a handful dried **cranberries** (optional)

1 **PUT** the cranberry juice in a saucepan and heat it for 2–3 minutes over
a medium heat. Add the sugar and sprinkle with the kanten, then
gently stir for 1–2 minutes until the sugar and kanten dissolve (do not
allow the mixture to boil). Set the pan aside for 10 minutes, but no
longer, because kanten sets in about 30 minutes at room temperature.

2 **CUT** the dragon fruit in half and carefully scoop out the flesh with
a melon baller, retaining the emptied shells to be used as serving cups.

3 **DIVIDE** the dragon fruit and grapes between the halved dragon fruit
shells and spoon the cranberry kanten over the fruit to fill each cup.
Leave to set at room temperature until ready to serve.

4 **SCATTER** a few dried cranberries around the dragon fruit, if you like,
and serve.

PEACH SNOW JELLIES WITH AZUKI

MOMO NO AWAYUKI-KAN TO YUDE AZUKI

**SERVES 4   PREPARATION TIME: 20 MINUTES, PLUS 4 HOURS SETTING
COOKING TIME: 2 HOURS, 10 MINUTES**

The Japanese normally eat fresh fruit for dessert, and fresh fruit jellies make an excellent alternative. The crunchy, sweet azuki complement the fluffy jelly in this dish wonderfully.

150g/5½oz canned **peaches**, drained

12g/½oz **gelatine** sheets, softened in warm water

5 tbsp **sugar**

1 tbsp **Cointreau**

red or green herbs, such as **shiso**

AZUKI BEANS:

90g/3¼oz/scant ½ cup dried **azuki beans**, soaked in water for 3–4 hours or overnight

100g/3½oz/scant ½ cup **sugar**

a pinch **salt**

1 **COOK** the azuki beans following step 2 on page 170, using 380ml/13fl oz/1½ cups water. Set aside to cool in the liquid.

2 **PURÉE** the peaches in a blender.

3 **DRAIN** the gelatine, put it in a saucepan with 150ml/5fl oz/scant ⅔ cup water and heat gently over a medium heat, stirring until the gelatine dissolves. Add the sugar and continue to stir until the sugar dissolves.

4 **TRANSFER** the hot gelatine liquid to a mixing bowl and whisk vigorously for 7–8 minutes until it becomes soft and fluffy. Place the bowl in a dish of ice-cold water and continue to whisk for another 7–8 minutes until it becomes completely snow white and firm. (This whisking makes the jelly beautifully smooth.) Mix in the puréed peaches and Cointreau and continue to whisk for 1 minute.

5 **POUR** the mixture into 4 individual cupcake moulds (about 190ml/6fl oz/¾ cup) and refrigerate for at least 4 hours until firmly set.

6 **SOAK** the moulds up to the rim in hot water, then turn the jellies out onto 4 plates. Using a slotted spoon, arrange the azuki beans around the snow jellies and serve with tiny tips of red or green herbs.

GINGER PEARS IN HOT PLUM SAUCE

NASHI NO PURAMU SOHSU SOE

SERVES 4 PREPARATION TIME: 20 MINUTES COOKING TIME: 45 MINUTES

Thanks to their beautiful red colour and slightly acidic taste, plums make an impressive as well as delicious sauce, which is further enhanced by the addition of fresh ginger.

5cm/2in piece **root ginger**, peeled and grated

2 tbsp **sugar**

4 not-too-ripe **pears** (any type), peeled

6 dark red **plums**

4 tbsp **golden syrup**

a handful **blueberries**

1 HEAT 250ml/9fl oz/1 cup water in a saucepan, mix in half of the grated ginger and the sugar and cook the pears over a gentle heat for about 10 minutes until just cooked. Transfer the pears and cooking liquid to a bowl, leaving 3 tbsp in the saucepan. Cover the pears and keep warm.

2 ADD the plums to the remaining liquid in the saucepan and simmer over a low heat for about 25 minutes until very soft. Remove from the heat and tip the contents into a fine-mesh sieve placed over a mixing bowl.

3 CRUSH the plums with a fork and discard the stones. Press the plums through the sieve with the back of a spoon to make a thin fruit purée; discard the skins.

4 SQUEEZE the remaining ginger in your hand to extract the juice. Put the plum purée in a saucepan and add the golden syrup and ginger juice. Warm gently over a medium heat, stirring a few times. Remove the pan from the heat and add the blueberries

5 DRAIN the pears, discarding the remaining liquid, and cut each pear in half lengthways. Arrange 2 halves on each of 4 plates and spoon 1–2 tbsp of the plum sauce on the side. Serve warm with the remaining sauce in a separate dish.

HOME-MADE ICE CREAM WITH JAPANESE FLAVOURS *JIKASEI AISUKURIMU WAFU FUMI SOE*

SERVES 4   PREPARATION TIME: 25 MINUTES, PLUS 5 HOURS FREEZING
COOKING TIME: 20 MINUTES

The two Japanese ingredients of matcha (powdered green tea) and ogura (sweet red beans used in the azuki paste) are commonly used to flavour ice cream, but in this recipe they are served within separate sauces. The vanilla ice cream is not as sweet as usual to compensate for the sweetness of the sauces.

150ml/5fl oz/scant ⅔ cup **milk**

3 tbsp **maple syrup**

1 **egg**, beaten

1 tsp **vanilla essence**

150ml/5fl oz/scant ⅔ cup **double cream**

MATCHA SAUCE:

80ml/2½fl oz/⅓ cup **double cream**

3 tsp **matcha**

2 tbsp **golden syrup**

OGURA SAUCE:

½ recipe quantity **Sweet Azuki Paste**
    (*see page 170*)

3 tbsp **golden syrup**

1 **HEAT** the milk and maple syrup in a saucepan over a medium heat until warm. Put the beaten egg in a large mixing bowl, then pour the milk mixture over, stirring continuously. Return the mixture to the pan and cook over a gentle heat for about 15 minutes, stirring continuously until the custard thickens. Strain the custard through a sieve and stir in the vanilla essence. Remove from the heat and leave to cool.

2 **WHIP** the cream until it forms soft peaks, then fold it into the custard. Pour into a freezer-proof container and freeze. Stir every 30 minutes with a fork until half-frozen (approximately 3 hours), then leave to freeze for a further 2 hours.

3 **MAKE** the matcha sauce by whipping the cream until it forms soft peaks, then gently stir in the matcha and syrup to make a smooth sauce.

4 **PREPARE** the ogura sauce by stirring the sweet azuki paste and syrup together until it is smooth.

5 **PLACE** 2–3 scoops of the ice cream in each of 4 dishes. Serve the ice cream with the 2 sauces.

CARAMEL-COATED SWEET POTATO

DAIGAKU IMO

**SERVES 4   PREPARATION TIME: 5 MINUTES, PLUS 10 MINUTES SOAKING
COOKING TIME: 15 MINUTES**

*Daigaku imo (meaning "university potato") is so called because it was created
to fill the stomachs of the young, cheaply and easily, and became very popular
among university students living away from home. This dish is eaten as a sweet
snack as well as a dessert.*

2 tbsp **sea salt**

3–4 **sweet potatoes,** about 700g/1½lb total
weight, halved lengthways and sliced into
1cm/½in thick half-moons

vegetable oil, for deep-frying

8 tbsp **sugar**

1 tsp **shoyu**

1 tbsp **black sesame seeds**

1 STIR the salt into 500ml/17fl oz/2 cups water and add the sweet potatoes.
Leave for 10 minutes, then drain and pat dry with kitchen paper.

2 HEAT the oil in a deep-fryer or wok to 100°C/200°F. Gently slide in
the potatoes and deep-fry over a medium heat, gradually increasing the
heat to a higher temperature, for 5–6 minutes until crisp and golden
brown. Remove the potatoes from the oil using a slotted spoon and
drain on a wire rack.

3 PUT the sugar and shoyu in a large saucepan with 5 tbsp water. Heat
over a medium heat for 5–6 minutes, stirring all the time, until the
mixture becomes syrupy. Remove from the heat and fold in the hot
fried potatoes.

4 DIVIDE the sweet potatoes between 4 plates, sprinkle with the sesame
seeds and serve hot.

PART 3

THE MENUS

*Planning a Japanese **meal** may seem daunting at first, but the following varied **collection** of menus will help to ensure everything goes smoothly, from the initial planning and timing to advance **preparation** and those important final touches. As with any other cuisine, a successful menu relies on a **balance** and variety of ingredients with a mix of flavours, **textures** and colours, which are all found in **abundance** in the following pages.*

*In Japan, consideration is also given to the **season** and the use of local produce. For instance, young green vegetables and **bamboo** shoots for spring; bonito tataki or **edamame** for early summer; mushrooms, chestnuts and **persimmon** for autumn; and hotpot dishes for winter. Seasonal flower petals or leaves are used to **decorate** dishes or the table.*

*Set the table with just a pair of hashi (chopsticks) and enjoy the **experience** of cooking and sharing **beautiful** Japanese food with your guests.*

SIMPLE LUNCH

FRIED RAMEN WITH MIXED SEAFOOD
(see page 166)

MISO SOUP WITH WAKAME AND TOFU
(see page 27)

CAULIFLOWER AND EDAMAME WITH WASABI DRESSING
(see page 136)

TIME PLAN

Noodles are a lunchtime favourite in Japan and these ramen noodles with mixed seafood are popular with both children and adults. Further enhanced by a soothing miso soup and a pretty salad, this is a truly simple, yet delicious and substantial menu.

The day before or in the morning, make the dashi stock for the miso soup. (Dashi can also be made well in advance and kept frozen for up to 3 months.) Serve the meal with cups of Japanese tea, if you like. Halve all the recipe ingredients to prepare this meal for two.

12.10 PM PREPARE and cook the cauliflower and edamame and marinate the cauliflower.

12.30 PREPARE the ingredients for the ramen. Make the miso soup and keep it warm.

12.50 COOK the noodles. Meanwhile, stir-fry the seafood and vegetables, then add them to the cooked noodles.

1.00 ASSEMBLE the cauliflower and edamame and serve with the ramen with mixed seafood and the miso soup.

PREPARATION NOTES

CHOOSE a very fresh cauliflower with a firm, white head and SEPARATE it into small, equal-sized florets, resembling pearls. REMOVE the miso soup from the heat just before it reaches boiling point to prevent it losing its flavour; keep warm with a lid on until ready to serve. PREPARE all the ingredients for the seafood ramen before starting to cook.

LUNCH BOX

TIME PLAN

SIMMERED PORK WITH KABOCHA

(see page 112)

GREEN BEANS WITH WHITE
DRESSING (without the dressing)

(see page 139)

FRUIT SALAD WITH GINGER
KANTEN (without the kanten and syrup)

(see page 174)

PLAIN BOILED JAPANESE RICE

(see page 24)

MISO PICKLES

(see page 30)

A delicious alternative to a sandwich, this Japanese bento box is made up of individual layers containing Japanese rice, succulent simmered pork with kabocha and red pepper, with a serving of green beans and some miso pickles. Fresh fruits refresh the palate.

Prepare the miso pickles in advance. The day before, make the simmered pork with kabocha, then leave to cool and refrigerate. You can use leftover rice from dinner but if the rice is to be freshly cooked, wash and soak in the measured water overnight and then cook in the morning. Use one-quarter of the ingredients for a single portion.

AM 7.00 COOK the rice (if not using leftovers), then arrange it in the bento box or container and leave to cool completely before adding other items or covering with a lid. While the rice is cooking, prepare and cook the beans as in step 2 of the recipe.

7.20 PREPARE the apple and persimmon, then put the apple in salty water as in step 4 of the recipe to prevent it discolouring. Drain the apple and pat dry.

8.00 DRAIN the pork dish so the juices do not run out of the box during transportation, then arrange in the box with the fine green beans and the miso pickles. Place the fruit in a separate container.

PREPARATION NOTES

BUY good-quality, lean, outdoor-reared pork for the main course. PREPARE the apple "rabbit's ears" for the fruit salad in advance, then, once they have been plunged into salty water to prevent discolouration, STORE in the fridge until you are ready to serve the fruit salad.

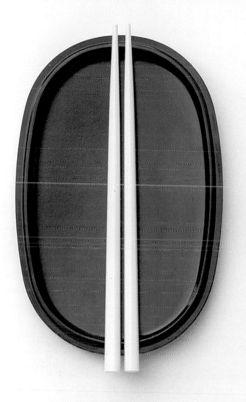

MID-WEEK LUNCH WITH FAMILY

Golden, crispy pork is traditionally served with finely shredded raw cabbage, which helps to refresh the palate. The healthy addition of simply simmered soya beans, pak choi and a beautiful red miso soup makes a colourful, attractive menu.

DEEP-FRIED PORK STEAK
(see page 116)

SQUASH MISO SOUP WITH TOFU AND MANGETOUT
(see page 67)

SIMMERED SOYA BEANS
(see page 147)

PAK CHOI AND BABY CLAMS IN MUSTARD DRESSING
(without the clams and dressing)
(see page 152)

PLAIN BOILED JAPANESE RICE
(see page 24)

10.45 AM
11.30
12.00 PM
12.15
12.30
12.50
1.00

The night before, soak the soya beans. Make the dashi stock for the soup. During the morning, wash the rice and leave to soak in the measured water until ready to cook. Serve the lunch with fresh fruit and green tea.

REMOVE the outer skin from the soaked soya beans and cook the beans in boiling water.

CUT up all the vegetables and the tofu. Steam the squash and cook the mangetout, then leave them to cool.

SEASON the beans and continue to cook them. Prepare the squash and miso mixture for the soup.

COOK the rice and keep it warm. Meanwhile, prepare the pork steaks and coat in the breadcrumbs. Heat the oil for deep-frying the pork.

ADD the carrot and konnyaku to the beans and continue to cook. Fry the pork steaks and keep them warm until ready to serve.

HEAT the dashi and complete the squash miso soup. Boil the pak choi following the method in step 1 of the recipe, then drain and keep warm.

SPOON the soup and soya beans into separate bowls. Arrange the pork and serving suggestions on plates and serve with the rice and pak choi all at the same time.

PREPARATION NOTES

BUY good-quality, thick-cut pork loin steaks and do not **SALT** too early, as the steaks will become tough if left salted for too long.

MID-WEEK LUNCH WITH FRIENDS

ASPARAGUS CHICKEN ROLLS
(see page 45)

SWORDFISH TERIYAKI WITH CELERY
(see page 127)

BROCCOLI SALAD WITH ANCHOVY SANBAIZU DRESSING
(see page 143)

PLAIN BOILED JAPANESE RICE "LOGS"
(see page 24)

SALT-PICKLED CHINESE LEAVES
(see page 29)

GINGER PEARS IN HOT PLUM SAUCE
(see page 181)

TIME PLAN

The starter and dessert can be made the day before, and the swordfish does not take long to cook, making this substantial menu ideal for a busy day's lunch party. The sanbaizu-dressed broccoli is the perfect partner for the terikayi, and the sweet but spicy pears round off the meal.

Make the pickled Chinese leaves up to 2 days in advance. The day before, make the asparagus chicken rolls up to step 4 of the recipe and store covered in the fridge. The dessert can also be made the day before, if liked, and the plum sauce reheated before serving.

AM 10.40 **WASH** the rice and leave to soak in the measured water. Prepare all the vegetables and fruit.

11.05 **POACH** the pears in the ginger mixture. Meanwhile, mix together the ingredients for the teriyaki marinade, then marinate the swordfish.

11.15 **REMOVE** the pears from the pan with all but 3 tbsp of the sauce, then cook the plums.

11.25 **COOK** the rice and keep warm. Boil the broccoli and cool under cold running water. Meanwhile, make the dressing for the salad.

11.40 **PURÉE** the plums and set aside.

11.55 **COOK** the celery, then the swordfish teriyaki; keep warm.

PM 12.25 **FRY** the chicken rolls, then add them to the dashi sauce and simmer. Meanwhile, make the rice "logs" and sprinkle with black sesame seeds.

12.45 **MAKE** the mustard sauce and cut the asparagus chicken rolls into slices. Spoon the dressing over the broccoli and watercress and stir to coat.

1.00 **ASSEMBLE** the savoury dishes in bento boxes or on plates and serve. Use the konbu to display the pickled Chinese leaves.

1.30 **MAKE** the plum sauce and add the blueberries, then arrange the dessert on plates and serve.

WEEKEND LUNCH WITH FAMILY

DEEP-FRIED MACKEREL AND STEAMED KABOCHA SQUASH

(see page 50)

MIXED SUSHI

(see page 91)

ASSORTED VEGETABLE SOUP

(see page 71)

HALF GONG PANCAKES

(see page 173)

PREPARATION NOTES

BUY really fresh mackerel and prawns and ask the fishmonger to prepare and fillet the mackerel for you. **KEEP** refrigerated or frozen dashi stock for future use.

TIME PLAN

The soup is quite substantial, so just a small amount is fine for this family lunch for four. The richness of the mackerel is complemented by simply cooked kabocha squash. Mixed sushi is a popular family dish, as are the half gong pancakes.

The day before, make the sweet azuki paste for the half gong pancakes, then refrigerate. Prepare the thin egg sheet for the mixed sushi. Make the dashi for the soup. Serve this lunch with cups of Japanese tea.

AM
10.15 **WASH** the rice and leave to soak in the measured water. Soak the shiitake for both the mixed sushi and soup. Prepare the rest of the ingredients for the mixed sushi and soup.

10.45 **COOK** the kabocha squash and all the vegetables for the mixed sushi.
11.15 **PREPARE** and marinate the mackerel. Cook the prawns for the mixed sushi.

11.45 **COOK** the rice. While the rice is cooking, make the pancake batter.
PM
12.15 **MAKE** the sushi rice, then assemble all the ingredients for the mixed sushi and cover with a clean dry tea towel.

12.30 **COOK** the soup and keep warm.
12.45 **DUST** the mackerel in flour, then deep-fry in batches.
1.00 **ARRANGE** and serve the mackerel with the kabocha, mixed sushi and the soup.
1.25 **MAKE** and assemble the pancakes, add the mint and serve when they have cooled.

WEEKEND LUNCH WITH FRIENDS

HAND-ROLLED SUSHI

(see page 83)

BEEF STEAK WITH SESAME MISO SAUCE

(see page 104)

CLEAR SOUP WITH CLAMS AND SOMEN NOODLES

(see page 75)

FRUIT SALAD WITH GINGER KANTEN

(see page 174)

PREPARATION NOTES

Buy **GOOD-QUALITY** steaks and take them out of the fridge at least 30 minutes before cooking to allow even cooking. **PREPARE** the aubergine and apple just before cooking or serving, because they will start to turn brown after being cut and peeled.

TIME PLAN

Hand-rolled sushi is perfect for a lunch with friends – it's not only simple to make but great fun for guests, as they get to make their own rolls. The richly flavoured beef comes with a sesame-infused sauce and is followed by a mouth-cleansing clear soup and refreshing fruit salad.

The ginger kanten takes only a short time to set, but you can make it the day before if you want to give yourself more time to prepare the rest of the lunch. As soon as you have a moment in the morning, wash the rice and leave it to soak in the measured water until ready to cook. Halve the quantity of ingredients specified in the sushi recipe if preparing this lunch for four people.

AM
11.00 **MAKE** the ginger kanten and leave to set, if not making it the day before. Make the sesame miso sauce for the steak.
11.20 **PREPARE** all the vegetables, except the aubergines, for the steak dish.
11.35 **MAKE** the konbu and saké stock for the soup and leave in the pan. Cook the rice for the sushi.
11.55 **SCRUB** the clams and cook the noodles for the soup. Refresh the noodles under cold running water.
PM
12.05 **PREPARE** the syrup and all the fruit for the fruit salad, except the apple. Cover and store in the fridge.
12.25 **SEASON** the sushi rice and transfer to a serving bowl. Prepare all the other ingredients for the sushi dish and arrange on serving plates.
12.50 **COMPLETE** the soup and keep warm, but do not add the noodles.
1.00 **SERVE** the hand-rolled sushi plate with rice, nori and lettuce.
1.25 **PREPARE** the aubergine. Pan-fry the steaks and vegetables and serve with the sesame miso sauce, then ladle the warm soup over the noodles and serve.
2.15 **PREPARE** the kanten and apple, assemble the fruit salad and serve.

SIMPLE DINNER

DEEP-FRIED TOFU WITH DASHI SAUCE

(see page 65)

GINGER PORK WITH ROCKET SALAD

(see page 115)

AVOCADO MISO SOUP WITH TOMATO AND TURNIP

(see page 68)

PLAIN BOILED JAPANESE RICE

(see page 24)

RICE BRAN PICKLES

(see page 30)

PREPARATION NOTES

HANDLE the avocado swiftly, as the beautiful pale green colour will turn brown if left peeled for too long. If you do not have time to make the Japanese rice bran pickles, **USE** gherkins and onions.

TIME PLAN

Deep-fried tofu served in a dashi sauce and simple ginger pork show the diversity of typical Japanese home cooking. The avocado miso soup is included to give this menu an interesting twist with its unusual flavour and colour. Serve with the rice bran pickles and plain rice.

If making the pickles from scratch, begin 6 days in advance. The day before, soak the konbu for the dashi soup stock. Freeze the pork steaks overnight, then half-defrost in the morning to make the meat much easier to slice thinly. When you have a moment during the day, wash the rice and leave to soak in the measured water until ready to cook.

PM

5.30 SLICE the pork and spread out on a plate to thaw completely if needed.

5.40 MAKE the dashi for the tofu dish as well as for the soup.

6.00 PREPARE the vegetables and grate the ginger for both the deep-fried tofu and the ginger pork. Make and dress the salad.

6.20 COOK the rice and leave covered with a lid. While the rice is cooking, press the tofu to remove excess water.

6.45 MIX together the ingredients for the ginger marinade and marinate the pork.

6.55 MAKE the avocado miso soup.

7.10 DEEP-FRY the tofu, and make the dashi sauce at the same time.

7.30 ASSEMBLE and serve the deep-fried tofu with dashi sauce.

7.45 STIR-FRY the pork, assemble with the salad and serve with the rice, pickles and avocado miso soup.

ROMANTIC DINNER

TARÉ-GRILLED SCALLOPS WITH VINEGARY SALAD
(see page 49)

SOUP-STEAMED DUCK
(see page 120)

ASPARAGUS WITH SESAME DRESSING
(see page 140)

RICE COOKED WITH CHESTNUTS
(see page 158)

PEACH SNOW JELLIES WITH AZUKI
(see page 178)

TIME PLAN

Golden taré-grilled scallops are followed by tender duck breasts simmered in a light broth and perfectly partnered by earthy chestnut rice and crisp, vibrant asparagus. The smooth snow jellies make a romantic finale.

The day before, prepare and cook the scallops following step 1 of the recipe; when cool, refrigerate. Prepare the peach snow jellies and cook the azuki beans. Halve the recipe ingredients to make this meal for two.

PM

5.15 WASH the rice and leave to soak in the measured water until ready to cook. Prepare all the vegetables. Make the asparagus with dressing.

5.45 COOK the chestnuts, then peel and cut into pieces.

6.00 COOK the duck and leave in the broth in the steamer.

6.45 COOK the chestnut rice and keep warm.

6.50 PREPARE the taré sauce and the salad for the scallops dish.

7.25 GRILL the scallops and assemble with the salad.

7.30 SERVE the scallops and salad with the pomegranate seeds.

7.50 MAKE the sauce for the duck. Meanwhile, slice the duck and arrange on plates with the cress. Spoon over a little of the sauce and serve with the chestnut rice and asparagus.

8.20 TURN out the peach snow jellies onto plates, add the azuki beans and serve.

PREPARATION NOTES

BUY very fresh, large, creamy-coloured scallops and cook with or without the orange coral still attached. If fresh chestnuts are not available, you can **COOK** the green pea or shimeji rice (see page 26) instead.

MID-WEEK DINNER WITH FAMILY

Gyoza, little dumplings filled with minced meat and vegetables, are ideal for the family to get involved in making, and the salmon hotpot makes a nutritious and sustaining main meal. The rice balls look quite stunning with their deep red azuki coating.

PAN-FRIED GYOZA

(see page 37)

SALMON HOTPOT

(see page 131)

GREEN BEANS WITH WHITE DRESSING

(see page 139)

RICE BALLS WRAPPED IN SWEET AZUKI PASTE

(see page 170)

The night before, soak the azuki beans in plenty of cold water and leave overnight. During the day when you have a moment, cook the rice and make the azuki paste for the dessert, then leave both to cool. This can also be done the day before.

PM

5.15 **DIVIDE** the rice into balls and wrap in the azuki paste, then leave, covered with a clean dry tea towel, until ready to serve.

5.45 **MAKE** the filling for the gyoza, then prepare them up to step 4.

6.10 **PREPARE** and cook the salmon hotpot. While the salmon is cooking, cook the green beans and make the white dressing.

6.45 **COOK** the gyoza.

7.00 **SERVE** the gyoza with the shoyu/rice vinegar dip and the chilli oil dip.

7.15 **HEAT** up the salmon hotpot and serve in individual bowls with the dressed green beans alongside.

7.45 **SERVE** the dessert on individual plates.

PREPARATION NOTES

BUY gyoza wrappers either chilled or frozen from oriental food shops. **START** pan-frying the gyoza just before serving as they are best eaten straightaway. Try to **GET** wild salmon rather than farmed fish, for texture and flavour.

MID-WEEK DINNER WITH FRIENDS

SEARED BEEF TATAKI
(*see page 34*)

TEMPURA
(*see page 135*)

SIMMERED VEGETABLES WITH CHICKEN
(*see page 119*)

PLAIN BOILED JAPANESE RICE
(*see page 24*)

HOME-MADE ICE CREAM WITH JAPANESE FLAVOURS
(*see page 182*)

PREPARATION NOTES
CHILL the plain flour for the tempura batter in the fridge overnight. **MAKE** sure there is ice-cold water in the fridge for the tempura batter.

Succulent marinated beef tataki starts this delightful menu of contrasting tastes and textures. It is followed by crisp tempura and typical Japanese assorted vegetables simmered with chicken. Plain rice serves as a perfect mouth-cleanser, while the ice cream is a refreshing finale.

The day before, make the ice cream and its sauces; keep the ice cream in the freezer and the sauces in the fridge. Make the beef tataki the day before or during the day and leave to marinate. During the day, wash the rice and soak in the measured water until ready to cook.

PM

5.45 **PREPARE** all the vegetables, ginger and serving suggestions. Soak the shiitake for the simmered vegetables. Cook the asparagus for the beef tataki and add to the beef marinade.

6.15 **MAKE** the tempura dipping sauce. Prepare the prawns and leave to dry on kitchen paper in the fridge.

6.45 **PREPARE** the chicken. Drain the shiitake and soak the lotus root. Stir-fry the chicken and vegetables.

7.00 **SLICE** the beef tataki, assemble with the asparagus and keep, covered, in the fridge. Make the sauce for the tataki.

7.15 **COOK** the rice; keep warm.

7.30 **SERVE** the beef tataki while the chicken and vegetables are simmering; keep warm.

7.45 **HEAT** the oil for deep-frying and prepare the tempura batter. Dust the prawns and vegetables with flour, then dip in the batter and deep-fry the tempura. Reheat the tempura dipping sauce.

8.25 **SERVE** the tempura, simmered vegetables with chicken and rice together. Remove the ice cream from the freezer to soften.

8.50 **SCOOP** the ice cream into dishes and serve with the sauces.

DINNER PARTY

Melt-in-the-mouth bonito sashimi and glorious prawn and egg terrine make impressive starters. Sukiyaki is perfect for an informal gathering, being both fun to make and nutritious, while the magical dragon fruit with cranberry kanten adds the finishing touch.

SEARED BONITO SASHIMI
(see page 96)

PRAWN AND EGG TERRINE
(see page 61)

SUKIYAKI
(see page 107)

PAK CHOI AND BABY CLAMS IN MUSTARD DRESSING
(see page 152)

RICE COOKED WITH SHIMEJI
(see page 26)

DRAGON FRUIT WITH CRANBERRY KANTEN
(see page 177)

The day before, make the prawn and egg terrine and pickled lotus flowers. Make the dashi. When you have a moment during the day, wash the rice and leave to soak in the measured water until ready to cook. If you are serving eight people, double all the quantities.

5.30 PM SEAR the bonito and make the dressing. Store separately, covered, in the fridge.

6.00 MAKE the dragon fruit with cranberry kanten and, when set, keep in the fridge.

6.15 CUT and prepare the beef, vegetables and tofu for the sukiyaki. Mix together the ingredients for the sukiyaki sauce in a jug. Arrange the sukiyaki ingredients on serving plates.

6.45 MAKE the pak choi and clams in mustard dressing.

7.15 COOK the shimeji rice and keep warm.

7.30 COMBINE the bonito tataki and the dressing, then arrange on plates with the daikon. Cut the terrine into slices and place on separate individual plates; serve both dishes together.

8.00 PLACE a portable gas or electric cooker on the dining table. Take the sukiyaki plates, beaten eggs and the sauce to the table. Diners help themselves to the ingredients and contribute to the cooking.

8.30 SERVE the shimeji rice and the pak choi and clams while still cooking and eating the sukiyaki.

9.00 SERVE the dragon fruit with cranberry kanten, sprinkled with some dried cranberries.

DRINKS PARTY

This selection of delectable morsels begins with the all-time favourite, grilled skewered chicken, followed by fresh vegetables with Japanese dips, an assorted selection of sushi and, finally, caramelized sweet potato.

GRILLED SKEWERED CHICKEN

(see page 38)

THREE DIPS WITH FRESH VEGETABLES

(see page 62)

THIN-ROLLED SUSHI

(see page 79)

MACKEREL LOG SUSHI

(see page 88)

CALIFORNIAN REVERSE ROLL

(see page 84)

CARAMEL-COATED SWEET POTATO *(see page 185)*

The day before, cut the chicken and vegetables for the grilled skewered chicken and store separately, covered, in the fridge. Salt the mackerel, then marinate in vinegar, drain and set aside, covered, in the fridge. Make the taré sauce. During the day, wash the rice for the sushi and soak in the measured water until ready to cook. These quantities will all serve eight to ten guests, with the exception of the chicken, which will need to have its ingredients doubled.

PM

3.00 **PREPARE** all the vegetables except the avocado and steam the kabocha for the vegetable dip. Soak the bamboo skewers for the chicken.

3.30 **COOK** the rice, then prepare the sushi rice and leave to cool.

4.00 **CUT** the smoked salmon and make the thin-rolled sushi. Set aside, uncut, covered with a clean dry tea towel.

5.00 **MAKE** the mackerel log sushi and set aside, uncut, in the cling film.

5.30 **PREPARE** the avocado, then make the Californian reverse rolls and set aside, uncut, in the cling film.

6.00 **THREAD** the chicken and vegetables onto skewers and set aside.

6.10 **MAKE** the three dips and arrange vegetables for dipping on large plates.

7.00 **PREHEAT** the grill to medium. Cut the rolled and mackerel sushi and arrange on a large serving plate with wasabi, pickled ginger and shoyu.

7.20 **GRILL** the chicken and vegetable skewers. While grilling, deep-fry the sweet potato, drain and set aside.

7.40 **SERVE** the skewers with the fresh vegetables and dips, then the assorted sushi. When ready, make the caramel and toss the fried sweet potatoes in it, then serve sprinkled with sesame seeds.

INDEX

A

abura-age 17
agar-agar 12
agedashi dofu 64
amazu shoga 28
ankou nabe 132
aomame gohan 26
asparagus
    asparagus chicken rolls 44, 194
    asparagus with sesame dressing 140, 202
asparagus no goma-ae 140
asparagus no sasami-maki 44
avocado miso soup with tomato and
    turnip 68, 201
azuki 10
    peach snow jellies with azuki 178, 202

B

bamboo shoots 10
battera 88
beef
    beef steak with sesame miso sauce 104, 198
    Japanese beef curry 108
    seared beef tataki 34, 206
    simmered beef with potato 110
    soup ramen with shredded beef 162
    sukiyaki 106, 209
beetroot soup rice with Japanese
    mushrooms 160

bonito 10
burokkori no anchobi sanbaizu-ae 142
broccoli salad with anchovy sanbaizu
    dressing 142, 194
butaniku no shoga-yaki 114
butaniku to kabocha no nitsuke 112

C

cauliflower and edamame with wasabi
    dressing 136, 189
celery
    enoki, cucumber and celery salad with
        vinaigrette 144
    swordfish teriyaki with celery
        126, 194
chawan-mushi 72
chicken
    asparagus chicken rolls 44, 194
    chicken balls with edamame 40
    deep-fried chicken with spring
        onion sauce 42
    grilled skewered chicken 38, 210
    rice bowl with chicken and egg 156
    rice bowl with minced chicken and
        scrambled egg 154
    simmered vegetables with chicken
        118, 206
Chinese leaves or cabbage 10
Chinese leaves, salt-pickled 29, 194

clams
    clear soup with clams and somen
        noodles 74, 198
    pak choi and baby clams in mustard
        dressing 152, 193, 209
cucumber
    cucumber cups 22
    enoki, cucumber and celery salad with
        vinaigrette 144
curry roux 10

D

daigaku imo 184
daikon 10
    chrysanthemum 20
daizu 17
 daizu no gomoku-ni 146
dashi 10, 27
dorayaki 172
doragon furutsu no kuranberi kenten soe 176
dragon fruit with cranberry kanten 176, 209
dried and pickled plums 11
dried bonito flakes 11
dried mixed sea vegetable salad 11
duck, soup-steamed 120, 202

E

ebi no kimi-soboro age 54
ebi no tamago-maki to kabu no hana 56

edamame 11
  cauliflower and edamame with
    wasabi dressing 136
  chicken balls with edamame 40
eggs
  clear soup with beaten egg 28
  Japanese thick omelette 31
  prawn and egg terrine 60, 209
  prawn egg rolls with radish flowers 56
  rice bowl with chicken and egg 156
  rice bowl with minced chicken and
    scrambled egg 154
  udon noodles in egg broth 168
enoki 11
enoki no sunomono 144
enoki, cucumber and celery salad with
  vinaigrette 144
equipment 23

F

fish
  fillets, slicing 19
  skinning 19
fish stock 27
fried ramen with mixed seafood 166,
  189
fruit salad with ginger kanten 174,
  190, 198
futo-maki 80

G

ginger 11
  fruit salad with ginger kanten 174, 190, 198
  ginger pears in hot plum sauce 180, 194
  ginger pork with rocket salad 114, 201
  pickled flowers 20
  vinegar-pickled ginger 28
gingko nut 11
ginnan 11
gohan 24
gomoku zushi 90
green beans with white dressing 138, 190, 205
gunniko no sengiri iri ramen 162
gyokai no zeri yose 46
gyoza, pan-fried 36, 205
gyoza wrappers 12
gyuniku no tataki 34

H

hakusai 10
  salt-pickled Chinese leaves 29, 194
  hakusai no shiozuke 29
half gong pancakes 172, 197
hamaguri to somen no sumashi-jiru 74
hanagatsuo 11
harusame vermicelli 12
hirame no sashimi salada 102
hiryozu 58
hiya-yakko salada umeboshi ae 150

hoso-maki 78
hotate no tare-yaki to sunomono 48

I

ice cream, home-made with Japanese
  flavours 182, 206
inari-zushi 92
iri-dori 118
ishikari nabe 130
iwashi no nanban-zuke 52

J

Japanese thick omelette 31
jikasei aisukurimu wafu fumi soe 182

K

kabocha squash 12
  deep-fried mackerel and steamed
    kabocha squash 50, 197
  simmered pork with kabocha 112, 190
kaisen yakisoba 166
kajiki-maguro no teriyaki selori soe 126
kakitama udon 168
kanten 12
kariforunia uramaki 84
katifurawa to edamame no wasabi-ae 136
katsuo 10
kenchin jiru 70
kezuribushi 11

kikurage 18
kinoko iri beet zousui 160
komé 14
kombu 12
konbu 12
konnyaku 12
kuri gohan 158

L

lotus root 13
    pickled flowers 20

M

mackerel
    deep-fried mackerel and steamed
        kabocha squash 50, 197
    mackerel log sushi 88, 210
    mackerel simmered in miso 122
mangetout 66, 193
masu no oshi-zushi 86
matcha 13
meat, slicing 22
medai no nimono satoimo soe 124
mirin 13
miso 13
    avocado miso soup with tomato and
        turnip 68, 201
    beef steak with sesame miso sauce 104,198
    mackerel simmered in miso 122

miso pickles 30, 190
miso soup with wakame and tofu 27, 189
    sea bass marinated in miso and grilled
        128
    squash miso soup with tofu and
        mangetout 66, 193
miso-juke 30
mitsuba 13
momo no awayuki-kan to yude azuki 178
monkfish shabu-shabu 132
mushi gamo 120
mushrooms
    beetroot soup rice with Japanese
        mushrooms 160
    enoki 11
    enoki, cucumber and celery salad with
        vinaigrette 144
    kikurage 18
    shiitake 16
    shimeji 16

N

nama yasia no dippu sanshu 62
nashi no puramu sohsu soe 180
nigiri zushi 76
niku-jaga 110
ninjin to sayaingen no shira-ae 138
nori 13
nuka zuke 30

O

ohagi 170
oyako donburi 156

P

pak choi and baby clams in mustard
    dressing 152, 193, 209
pakuchoi to asari no karashi-ae 152
pancakes
    gyoza wrapper 11
    half gong pancakes 172, 197
peach snow jellies with azuki 178, 202
pears
    ginger pears in hot plum sauce 180,
        194
pickled daikon 14
pickles
    miso pickles 30, 190
    rice bran pickles 30, 201
pork
    deep-fried pork steak 116, 193
    ginger pork with rocket salad 114, 201
    simmered pork with kabocha 112, 190
prawns
    golden prawns 54
    handling 19
    prawn and egg terrine 60, 209
    prawn egg rolls with radish flowers 56
    tofu and prawn balls 58

R

radish
  daikon 10
  pickled flowers 20
ramen 14
  fried ramen with mixed seafood 166, 189
  soup ramen with shredded beef 162
red snapper, simmered with satoimo 124
renkon 13
rice 14
  beetroot soup rice with Japanese
    mushrooms 160
  plain boiled 24, 190, 193-4, 201, 206
  rice balls wrapped in sweet azuki
    paste 170, 205
  rice bowl with chicken and egg 156
  rice bowl with minced chicken and
    scrambled egg 154
  rice cooked with chestnuts 158, 202
  rice cooked with peas 26
  rice cooked with shimeji 26, 209
  sushi 24
rice vinegar 14

S

saba no miso-ni 122
saba no tatsuta-age to mushi kabocha 50
saké 15
salmon hotpot 130, 205

sansho 15
sardines
  deep-fried sardines marinated in
    spicy sauce 52
sashimi
  assorted 94
  mackerel sashimi with sea
    vegetables 98
  pressed sea bass sashimi
    hakata-style 100
  seared bonito 96, 209
  turbot sashimi with salad 102
sashimi moriawase 94
satoimo 15
  simmered red snapper with satoimo 124
scallops
  taré-grilled scallops with vinegary
    salad 48, 202
sea bass marinated in miso and grilled 128
seafood in jelly 46
sesame seeds 15
seven-spice chilli powder 16
shichimi 16
shiitake 16
shime saba to kaiso salada 98
shimeji 16
shimeji gohan 26
shin katsuo no tataki 96
shirataki 16

shiso 16
shouga kenaten no furutsu salada 174
shoyu 17
soba 17
  soba noodles with tempura 164
soboro donburi 154
somen 17
  clear soup with clams and somen
    noodles 74, 198
soup
  assorted vegetable soup 70, 197
  avocado miso soup with tomato and
    turnip 68, 201
  beetroot soup rice with Japanese
    mushrooms 160
  clear soup with beaten egg 28
  clear soup with clams and somen
    noodles 74, 198
  miso soup with wakame and tofu 27, 189
  soup ramen with shredded beef 162
  squash miso soup with tofu and
    mangetout 66
  steamed egg custard soup 72
soya beans 17
  simmered soya beans 146, 193
squash
  deep-fried mackerel and steamed
    kabocha squash 50, 197
  kabocha 12

squash miso soup with tofu and
    mangetout 66, 193
su 14
sukiyaki 106
sumeshi 24
sushi
    Californian reverse roll 84, 210
    fried tofu parcel 92
    hand-moulded 76
    hand-rolled 82, 198
    mackerel log 88, 210
    mixed sushi 90, 197
    pressed sushi with smoked trout 86
    thick-rolled 80
    thin-rolled 78, 210
susuzi no miso-yaki 128
suzuki no hakata-oshi 100
sweet potato, caramel-coated 184, 210
swordfish teriyaki with celery 126, 194

T

takuan 14
tamago no sumashi jiru 28
tamago shinjo to hasu no amasu-zuke, kinusaya soe 60
tamago-taki 31
temaki zushi 82
tempura 134, 206
    soba noodles with tempura 164
tempura soba 164

thin deep-fried tofu 17
three dips with fresh vegetables 62, 210
tofu 17
    abura-age 17
    deep-fried tofu with dashi sauce 64, 201
    fried tofu parcel sushi 92
    miso soup with wakame and tofu 27, 189
    squash miso soup with tofu and
        mangetout 66, 193
    tofu and prawn balls 58
    tofu salad with umeboshi dressing 150
tofu to kinusaya no kabocha misoshiru 66
tomato to kabu no abokado misoshiru 68
tomatoes
    avocado miso soup with tomato and
        turnip 68, 201
tonkatsu 116
tonkatsu sauce 18
tori no kara-age negi sosu-ae 42
tori shinjo to edamame 40
tuna 18
turnips
    avocado miso soup with tomato and
        turnip 68, 201
    turnip flowers 20

U

udon 18
    udon noodles in egg broth 168

umeboshi 11
    tofu salad with umeboshi dressing 150

V

vegetables
    cutting 22
    simmered assorted 148
    simmered vegetables with chicken
        118, 206
    three dips with fresh vegetables 62, 210

W

wafu beef curry 108
wakame 18
    miso soup with wakame and tofu 27, 189
wakame to tofu no miso shiru 27
wasabi 18
    cauliflower and edamame with
        wasabi dressing 136, 189
wood ear fungus 18

Y

yaki gyoza 36
yakitori 38
yasia no nishime 148